THE FAITH OF ROBERT BROWNING

by the same author

THE BEATITUDES
THE CLAIMS OF CHRIST
LUKE'S PORTRAIT OF JESUS
THE MEANING OF THE OLD TESTAMENT
THE PARABLES OF THE GOSPELS
PAUL'S LETTERS TO HIS FRIENDS
PURITANISM AND RICHARD BAXTER
THEY WROTE OUR HYMNS

editor:

THE HOLY COMMUNION
A TREASURY OF CHRISTIAN VERSE
A BOOK OF PRAYERS FOR SCHOOLS
etc.

The Faith of
Robert Browning

HUGH MARTIN
C.H., D.D.

SCM BOOK CLUB
NAPERVILLE, ILL.

Copyright of frontispiece:
Radio Times Hulton Picture Library

FIRST PUBLISHED 1963
© SCM PRESS LTD 1963
PRINTED IN GREAT BRITAIN BY
BILLING AND SONS LTD
GUILDFORD AND LONDON

CONTENTS

I · Poet and Prophet · 7

II · The Life Story · 25

III · The Eternal Purpose · 41

IV · God in Christ · 63

V · The Mystery of Evil · 83

VI · After Death? · 95

VII · The Ring and the Book · 106

VIII · His Reverie · 120

Books on Browning · 124

Indexes · 125

I

Poet and Prophet

> It is the glory and good of Art
> That Art remains the one way possible
> Of speaking truths, to mouths like mine at least.
> *The Ring and the Book*

For some fifty years two large portraits have hung beside my study desk, visible whenever I lift my eyes. One is of my father, to whom I owe an incalculable debt, paternally, intellectually, and spiritually: the other is of Robert Browning. That, I suppose, dates me in more ways than one. The other day a friend was speaking to me about a well-known minister. 'He's an old-fashioned type,' he said. 'You know; he quotes Browning in the pulpit.'

Can it be more than a rear-guard action for a lost cause to be writing a book about Robert Browning in this year of grace? He is dismissed as being obscure, full of uncouth rhymes and prosaic lines. He is an 'optimist'; a grave charge to bring against any man these days. He is a Victorian. He preaches: he has a 'message'. One contemporary poet and critic, whom it would perhaps be kinder not to name, admits grudgingly that it must be conceded that in some senses Browning is 'a major poet, but a poet only in the lowest sense in which it is possible to use the word at all'.

We must consider the counts in this formidable indictment. There are, nevertheless, some signs that the reaction against

Victorian poetry, just because it is the work of a recent generation and necessarily out of date, has nearly spent itself. People are more ready to form a balanced judgment of its worth. At any rate let me confess at once that I have no doubt at all that Browning is among the very greatest of our poets, to be read for the sheer pleasure of it, for the loveliness and understanding of his writings, and for his deep insight into human nature and into God's ways with men.

I

It must be admitted that he was Victorian, at least in the sense that his life-time, 1812 to 1889, practically spanned the Victorian era at both ends. He was a younger contemporary and acquaintance of Wordsworth and a close friend of Dickens and of Thomas Carlyle. (He found Mrs Carlyle 'a hard, unlovable woman', but perhaps their relations were strained because once in the fervour of an argument he set down a boiling kettle in the middle of her hearth rug!) He was on the most cordial terms with Tennyson, and together they became the outstanding figures of Victorian literature. But it is in fact very doubtful if Browning was ever a *good* Victorian. He wrote like a realist fifty years before realism was in fashion, and before people were ready to accept it, and he suffered in consequence, as Thomas Hardy did. He proclaimed the doctrine of evolution long before the publication of Darwin's *Origin of Species*, when it was a storm centre of controversy. He did not trade in sugar and sentiment or try in the least to accommodate himself to popular taste. The Victorians, in fact, did not like him and he had to wait many years for any public recognition.

The charge of obscurity has also something in it, and it has frightened many people from giving his writings a fair trial. Though he certainly did not write obscurely with intention, he had no ambition to be 'the idle singer of an empty day', in the phrase of William Morris. Poetry to him was more than a cultured amusement, certainly never an opiate or a tranquillizer. 'I can have little doubt,' he wrote to a friend in 1872, 'that my writing has been in the main too hard for many I should have been pleased to communicate with, but I have never designedly tried to puzzle people, as some of my critics have supposed. On the other hand I have never pretended to offer such literature as should be a substitute for a cigar or a game of dominoes to an idle man.'

When Ruskin complained of the difficulties in *Men and Women* he replied: 'I cannot begin writing poetry till my imaginary reader has conceded licences to me which you demur at altogether. I *know* that I don't make out my conception by my language: all poetry being a putting of the infinite within the finite. You would have me paint it all plain out, which can't be . . . You ought, I think, to keep pace with the thought, tripping from ledge to ledge of my "glaciers", as you call them; not stand poking your alpenstock into the holes and demonstrating that no foot could have stood there: suppose it sprang over there?'[1]

Much of the trouble, where there is obscurity, is due to the reader failing 'to keep pace with the thought'. 'He never thinks but at full speed,' Swinburne wrote of him.[2] His mind worked too rapidly for his pen, too rapidly for the slower minds of his readers. He tries at times, as did Shakespeare, Donne and Manley Hopkins, to get too much into the space. A new thought treads upon the heels of the first; illustrations, analogies and metaphors pour out in superabundance. The poem, and his readers, would often get on better if there were fewer of them.

[1] Quoted in John Bryson, *Robert Browning*, an admirable short introduction.
[2] *George Chapman: A Critical Essay*.

Some of the poems on the Greek classics, *Prince Hohenstiel-Schwangau*, *Fifine at the Fair*, and some of the shorter lyrics, none of them among his greatest, demand careful reading: and *Sordello* above all. Everyone knows Tennyson's joke, that he could only understand two lines of *Sordello*, the first and the last, and they were both untrue: 'Who will may hear Sordello's story told' and 'Who would has heard Sordello's story told.' The trouble with *Sordello* mainly arose from his over-sensitive reaction (he was only twenty-three) to criticisms of his earlier poems, *Pauline* and *Paracelsus*, as being too wordy and diffuse. So he took care this time to cut out all the unnecessary words, and sometimes necessary ones went too. *Sordello* also suffers from his tendency to overdo the 'local colour'. In wide-ranging research he had accumulated stores of information about the architecture, politics and daily life of thirteenth century Italy. His less erudite readers do not understand the allusions and would not be interested if they did. Inability to select the essential and the telling is a usual mark of the inexperienced writer. In later years Browning deprecated people puzzling their heads over what he dismissed as an immature work, which he once tried unavailingly to rewrite. Present day readers can leave it alone without great loss; though T. S. Eliot rather surprisingly names *Sordello* and *The Ring and the Book* as his two greatest poems. Let us admit that Browning is guilty at times of irritating parentheses and uncompleted sentences. There are places where it seems that a little more care in tidying up the text would have made a great deal of difference. Some undeniable obscurity there is, but it has been grossly exaggerated. Most of his poems are as lucid as great poetry can ever be, and 'obscurity' has too often become a parrot cry uttered by those with little first hand knowledge.

Related to this complaint is the one about his uncouth and

POET AND PROPHET

strange vocabulary and his harsh rhymes. Donne in his younger days broke rudely and cynically into the sentimentalism of much Elizabethan love poetry: 'For God's sake hold your tongue and let me love', he cried. That might have been written by Browning, and for the same reason: he wanted to get away from sentimentality. He was deliberately colloquial. Sometimes his poetry is like the clever talk of a man who doesn't always finish, or need to finish, his sentences. Sometimes he is vulgar and rough because he is speaking in character, 'rudely, the verse being in the mood it paints', as he says in *Pauline*. The very nature of his psychological studies, speaking in the person of another, often an ignorant country bumpkin or a crook, demands that he should use rough, vulgar slang and not 'prettify'.

Some of his grotesque rhyming was done just for the fun of it. He must have chuckled over many of his lines. Once at a dinner party he was challenged to produce a rhyme for rhinoceros, which he delightedly did, and even, for Tennyson's amusement, rhymes for Ecclefechan and Craigenputtock! All this gave him great pleasure, and why not? Here is a fairly mild example from *Pachiarotto*:

> He tried to make obedient
> The wolf, fox, bear and monkey,
> By piping advice in one key—
> That his pipe should play a prelude
> To something heaven-tinged not hell-hued,
> Something not harsh but docile,
> Man-liquid not Man-fossil.

For some subjects of a satirical, ironic or humorous type, this is entirely appropriate and we can share the fun. The pity is that he sometimes used this manner for unsuitable themes. And it must be admitted that we do not nowadays appreciate all of his humour. Some of the jokes seem thin and tasteless. Nothing changes more quickly than the fashion in jokes, as can be proved by looking at back volumes of *Punch*. What is more tedious than many of the alleged comic interludes in Shakespeare's plays, where the actors of today pathetically slap their thighs and one another's backs and laugh vociferously, as if to prove that they at least see the point of the joke?

Much modern poetry, painting and sculpture is grotesque, harsh, disjointed, because, I suppose, the artist sees life that way. I find much of it as incomprehensible as anything in Browning. Indeed I wonder if some of Browning's own grotesque grimness may not be due to something of the same feeling. At least he found the world full of tragedy and wrestled with the cruelty and apparent meaningless of life. A mysterious poem that seems to offer itself for this kind of examination is *Childe Roland to the Dark Tower came*, and several critics have taken a hand in interpreting it. Browning himself denied that it meant anything in particular: it was just a story suggested by a line in *King Lear* and a picture he had seen; it 'came upon me as a kind of dream', he said, and he did not know what he meant by it.[1] But his denial proves nothing, as any psychoanalyst will tell you. We must accept his assurance that no allegory was intended and not attempt to give a name to the dark tower, the blind horse or the 'hateful cripple'. The whole poem has an eerie quality, and the intensity of feeling of a nightmare. It tells of the journey of a solitary knight through a no man's land, a 'waste land', a desolation so dreadful that nothing short of the Day of Judgment could clear it up, a journey in which there is no return. I am no psychoanalyst, but without going to the extremes of some writers, it seems to me that Browning here is seeing life as a pilgrimage through a grim and terrible world, strewn with the wreckage of past lives, and yet a world through which man must

[1] *A Browning Handbook*, De Vane, p. 204.

press on with a stout heart, ready to the very last to sound his horn of challenge to the unknown.[1] That after all is what Browning openly and consciously said in many poems, and notably in *Prospice* (see page 104). Childe Roland lived to tell the tale: Browning emerged with a faith. Perhaps he can speak to the present generation.

2

To admit that Browning is at times deliberately uncouth and even ugly in style and words, must not be allowed to hide from us that he is one of the greatest metrical masters in English literature. No poet has used a greater variety of metrical forms and none has been more skilful in their handling. If sometimes he sacrificed form to content, he could sing when he wanted to. Some poets, such as Swinburne, have been so concerned with form that they have sacrificed content. Browning could write the most exquisite lyrics, and often did. It is ridiculous to charge him with not caring about form and beauty, but he believed, rightly or wrongly, that there were times when matter must control form. In poetry substance and form cannot finally be separated. The 'message' must be fitly clothed if it is to be literature at all. In true poetry both are inextricably welded together. This welding at white heat Browning did not always achieve; but many times he did. He certainly has some dreadful lines. Those who want them can also dig them out of Tennyson,

[1] *Childe Roland* is a little reminiscent of the adventure of that other pilgrim recorded by John Bunyan, 'the object of my utmost admiration and reverence', as Browning wrote to a correspondent who had written to him about his poem, 'Ned Bratts', which is based on a story in Bunyan's *Life and Death of Mr Badman*, and brings in Bunyan and his blind daughter. A portrait of Bunyan hung in Browning's London study, beside those of Milton and Spenser. See *New Letters of Robert Browning*, ed. De Vane and Knickerbocker 1951, pp. 251ff. For his sense of the tragedy of life see further in Chapter V, 'The Mystery of Evil'.

Wordsworth, Byron or Shelley: perhaps there is no great poet who has not left in his works many dull and lifeless passages. Browning certainly has stretches of prose divided into decasyllables, yet his mastery of blank verse, in variety, ease, liveliness, grace, can be seen in *The Ring and the Book*. In a great variety of metres he can show passages and whole poems which for sheer technique can stand comparison with anything in English, as I trust the quotations in this book will demonstrate, though they will mostly be chosen for other reasons.

Many of Browning's really good poems suffer from their undue length. Like Gladstone, in Disraeli's famous indictment, he was apt to be 'inebriated with the exuberance of his own verbosity'. There are some poems we could do without altogether: but of which of our poets could that not be said?

3

We have been travelling on the brink of the issue as to whether a poet ought to have a 'message' at all. Browning thought he had. And when at last he achieved national and international recognition in the eighteen-seventies and eighties it was not only for the skill and interest of his poems but because the Victorian world had at last come to believe that he had something of great moment to say. The substance of that message is the main theme of later chapters of this book, but two previous questions must be examined first. Is it legitimate for a poet to have a 'message'? If it is, have we any right to interpret the works of a 'dramatic' poet like Browning as expressing his own beliefs?

Ought a poet to have a message? In 1852 Browning wrote an introduction to a volume of letters by Shelley. The letters were proved spurious and the volume was withdrawn, but his estimate of Shelley and of the nature of the poet's task both remain of

POET AND PROPHET

interest. He distinguishes between two kinds of poet, the *fashioner* of objective scenes and people, independent of his own personality, which he leaves others to interpret if they wish; and the *seer*, who seeks to present imaginatively his conception of truth. Shelley can be both, though he is mostly a seer; and mankind needs both. A true understanding of Shelley, says Browning in his not very lucid way, sees his work as a 'sublime, fragmentary essay towards a presentation of the correspondency of the universe to Deity, of the natural to the spiritual, of the actual to the ideal. Poetry is concerned not only with artistic presentation but with ethical and spiritual vision.'[1]

We may follow this clue further. A distinction is to be drawn, however difficult, between the poet as a story-teller and imaginative artist, the lyric painter of a mood, and the poet, perhaps the same poet, as a thinker, a critic of life and its meaning. Milton, for example, is both, though it might be argued that he is at his greatest when he forgets his avowed intention 'to justify the ways of God to men'. At times he is grappling with problems and appealing to our intellects. At others the story is everything; the heart and the imagination are called into play—and then Satan is apt to capture our sympathies! Milton's theology is detachable from his story, as Spenser's lumbering allegory is separable from the poetic story of *The Faerie Queene*. In *Samson Agonistes* he is again both propagandist and imaginative creator. Samson is vividly drawn, 'eyeless in Gaza, at the mill with slaves', 'fallen on evil days'. But he is also drawing John Milton, whose own Philistine first wife had betrayed his dreams, and who has seen the cause for which he ventured all and gave his sight, defeated.

[1] In passing, it is interesting to note that Browning held that before he died Shelley had moved from doctrinaire atheism to theism. 'I shall say what I think,' adds Browning, 'had he lived he would have finally ranged himself with the Christians.'

Poetry may be written to persuade readers to accept the poet's opinions. Or it may be descriptive in memorable words of a scene, an event or a mood. But some poetry does not lend itself to logical analysis. Its imagery may say something to us of beauty and mystery even if we cannot translate it into prose. It may bring us to 'magic casements, opening on the foam of perilous seas, in faery lands forlorn'.[1] Browning has poetry of all three kinds.

In *Heroes and Hero Worship* Carlyle insists that 'at all times Prophet and Poet, well understood, have much kindred of meaning'. They have penetrated into the mystery of the universe, 'and it is their business to reveal it to us.' 'It is a man's sincerity and depth of vision that makes him a poet.' Poetry is 'musical thought' and 'the poet is he who *thinks* in that manner'. The prophet—may we not say?—is not concerned with the form in which the truth is uttered, so long as he is able to communicate with his hearer. The poet, as poet, is concerned to clothe the truth in a vesture of beauty and power. The same man may be both poet and prophet and the greatest poets at their greatest moments fuse both functions into one. Leslie Stephen, in his *Encyclopedia Britannica* article, thinks Browning did not always know if he was writing poetry or versifying logic. Yet, writes Henry Jones, there are times when 'his convictions catch fire and truth becomes beauty for him: not beauty truth, as with Keats or Shelley'. 'It is not when he argues that Browning proves: it is when he sees as a poet sees.'[2]

Before they had even met, Elizabeth Barrett hailed him as 'poet and prophet',[3] and that is how Browning thought of himself, though with all modesty. To the end of his days he sincerely

---
[1] Keats, *Ode to the Nightingale*.
[2] Henry Jones, *Browning as a Philosophical and Religious Teacher*, p. 16.
[3] William Sharp, *Robert Browning*, p. 139.

POET AND PROPHET

maintained the superiority of the poetry of Tennyson and of his wife to his own. But he did believe he had a message. The curious title, *Bells and Pomegranates,* of the series of booklets in which he published some of his poems, is revealing. Browning said the reference was to the embroidered hem of the High Priest's garment described in Ex. 28.33f., which following one rabbinic interpretation, he took to symbolize music and thought, the two elements he sought to unite. At least in his early days he had as lofty a view of the poet's calling as a dedicated being, as ever the young Milton had.

4

But is it possible to discover what his message was? To take a quotation out of context is always dangerous. 'Shakespeare says' is as risky a statement as 'the Bible says'. It is illegitimate to quote speeches by Macbeth as his creator's own judgment on the meaning of life.

> As flies to wanton boys are we to the gods;
> They kill us for their sport.

That is natural on the lips of the blind, broken Duke of Gloster in *King Lear,* but we must not quote it as the belief of Shakespeare. To estimate what Shakespeare thought about Christianity is a difficult task. It is not evidence to quote, as has often been done, what Henry IV says about the Crusade:

> To chase these pagans in those holy fields
> Over whose acres walked those blessed feet,
> Which fourteen hundred years ago were nailed
> For our advantage, on the bitter cross.

That is what Henry fittingly would say.

A similar problem arises with Robert Browning. More than

once, for example in *House,* he protested against the gossip hunters who tried to pry into his personal life or draw deductions about himself from his poetry. He often repeated what he said in the preface to the reissue of *Pauline* in 1888, that his poetry was 'always dramatic in principle, and so many utterances of so many imaginary persons, not mine'. His most characteristic poems put men and women of his own creation, though often with some historical reality, into their own age and setting. Then he stood back to watch how they thought and acted and what sort of people they really were. I have read that characters invented by novelists and dramatists often seem to their creators to take the initiative and follow their own unexpected ways, and we may guess that Browning's men and women often came alive like that. All too often, 'Browning says' introduces a quotation from some character created by him but very unlike him, such as the worldly and cynical Don Juan in *Fifine at the Fair,* who utters some admirable sentiments in the course of his rationalizations. It would be as legitimate to hold Browning responsible for his Caliban's theology as for his Don Juan's views on married fidelity.

In *At the Mermaid* Browning protests in the character of Shakespeare against those who claim to read the dramatist's soul in his writings.

> Here's the work I hand, this scroll,
>   Yours to take or leave; as duly,
>   Mine remains the unproffered soul.
>   . . . .
> Which of you did I enable
>   Once to slip inside my breast,
> There to catalogue and label
>   What I like least, what love best,
> Hope and fear, believe and doubt of,
>   Seek and shun, respect—deride?

POET AND PROPHET

Nevertheless the disclaimer was more true for Shakespeare than for Browning—though perhaps Wordsworth had some right to say even of Shakespeare that in the sonnets at least he did 'unlock his heart'. For Browning did at times speak for himself and reveal his beliefs. The poems in which he speaks completely without disguise are few; partially in *Easter Day*, wholly in *Christmas Eve, La Saisiaz, Ferishtah's Fancies, One Word More*, and in much of *Paracelsus* and *Saul*, and in the Pope's soliloquy in *The Ring and the Book*. But what a wealth is here! And if in a poet's work a point of view appears repeatedly in different disguises, it is not unreasonable to see in it a view of the writer himself, especially if it turns up again in a poem in which he is avowedly speaking in person: there are also letters and records of conversations. We must certainly proceed with caution, but Browning did sometimes 'unlock his heart'.

5

It is worth pausing longer here with those 'dramatic' writings to which reference has been made. The word is ambiguous because it suggests stage plays. Browning did indeed write a number of plays, several of which were performed on the stage; *Strafford* at Covent Garden, *A Blot in the 'Scutcheon* at Drury Lane, and *Colombe's Birthday* at the Haymarket. They were by no means the failures they are sometimes represented to have been. On the whole they were well received, but they were haunted by such misfortunes as unsuitable casting, inadequate rehearsing, blunders in production, and the defection of a leading actor at the last minute, culminating in Browning's quarrel with Macready, the well-known actor-manager, which made him vow to write no more plays. With all that we are not now concerned. The sorry story is told at length in Mrs Orr's *Life*, where it is made clear that the faults were not all on one side. Whether or not Browning could have become a good playwright, there is no doubt about his brilliance as a dramatic writer in the broader sense of one who creates characters. In his long series of dramatic monologues he created a substantially new literary form. The titles of many of his volumes tell their own story: *Dramatic Lyrics, Dramatic Romances and Lyrics, Men and Women, Dramatis Personae, Dramatic Idyls*. Many of his works not in these books are of the same genre.

Browning had a remarkable gift of getting inside a character to see life as they might see it; a repulsive person like Guido or Caliban or Sludge, or a very different personality such as Cleon or the Pope. He set them to speak for themselves in a vividly drawn setting, often at a moment of crisis in their lives, in a state of inner conflict and tense feeling. The tragedy and comedy of human life is depicted in unforgettable fashion through an astonishing variety of men and women, in a gallery rivalled only by that of Shakespeare.

Browning's people come from many lands and ages; ancient Athens and the world of cultured paganism; the Middle Ages and the Renaissance both in their glory and in their disgrace; Russia, Italy, France, Spain, America and England. Arthur Symons has described their far-reaching variety in a remarkable sentence: 'The men and women who live and move in that new world of his creation are as varied as life itself; they are kings and beggars, saints and lovers, great captains, poets, painters, musicians, priests and popes, Jews, gipsies and dervishes, street girls, princesses, dancers with the wicked witchery of the daughter of Herodias, wives with the devotion of the wife of Brutus, joyous girls and malevolent greybeards, statesmen, cavaliers, soldiers of humanity, tyrants and bigots, ancient sages and modern spiritualists, heretics, scholars, scoundrels, devotees, rabbis, persons of quality and men of low estate, men and women

POET AND PROPHET

as multiform as nature or society has made them.'[1] He might indeed, be described as a 'human nature poet', in the same kind of way that Wordsworth is often called a nature poet. Men and women were his subject.

6

None the less he was a keen observer of nature and a great lover of animals. He has some magnificent descriptions of scenery on the large scale, observed not invented, as well as exquisite miniatures of the near-at-hand, flowers and mosses and waterfalls. A host of birds and beasts, faithfully watched, move through his world. He has a keen eye for colour. Fra Lippo Lippi is certainly not to be identified with him, but in his artist's view of the world he speaks for his creator:

> You've seen the world
> —The beauty and the wonder and the power,
> The shapes of things, their colours, lights and shades,
> Changes, surprises,—and God made it all!
> —For what? Do you feel thankful, ay or no,
> For this fair town's face, yonder river's line,
> The mountain round it and the sky above,
> Much more the figures of man, woman, child,
> These are the frame to? What's it all about?
>
> . . . .
>
> This world's no blot for us,
> Nor blank; it means intensely, and means good:
> To find its meaning is, my meat and drink.

Nature, as in a famous passage in *Paracelsus*, is an expression of the creative joy of God who is master of it and above it, rather than the 'Presence deeply interfused' of Wordsworth.[2] Nature is not personified nor is his approach sentimental. There is little

[1] *Introduction to the Study of Browning*, p. 9f.
[2] See p. 49 below.

trace of the 'pathetic fallacy': Nature does not feel with man. It is rather a background for human life and acquires its true meaning only when man arrives to give it a voice, consciousness and self-expression. Man comes at the crown of the ages-long evolutionary process.

Once arrived man imprints, says *Paracelsus*,

> His presence on all lifeless things: the winds
> Are henceforth voices, wailing or a shout,
> A querulous mutter or a quick gay laugh,
> Never a senseless gust now man is born.
> The herded pines commune and have deep thoughts,
> A secret they assemble to discuss
> When the sun drops behind their trunks which glare
> Like grates of hell: the peerless cup afloat
> Of the lake-lily is an urn, some nymph
> Swims bearing high above her head: no bird
> Whistles unseen, but through the gaps above
> That let light in upon the gloomy woods,
> A shape peeps from the breezy forest-top,
> Arch with small puckered mouth and mocking eye.
> The morn has enterprise, deep quiet droops
> With evening, triumph takes the sunset hour,
> Voluptuous transport ripens with the corn
> Beneath a warm moon like a happy face:
> —And this to fill us with regard for man.

This, be it noted, is not how things *are* but how they are pictured in man's imagination. The nymph is not really there. The pines do not take counsel. This is man's 'Let's pretend'. Nature for Browning can be a back-drop for human passion, but there is seldom a hint of the interpenetrating of man and nature seen in so many poets.

Yet how carefully and beautifully that back-drop is painted. Take this description at the beginning of *Pippa Passes*, where sun-rise floods the world with glory:

POET AND PROPHET

Day!
Faster and more fast,
O'er night's brim, day boils at last:
Boils, pure gold, o'er the cloud-cup's brim
Where spurting and suppressed it lay,
For not a froth-flake touched the rim
Of yonder gap in the solid gray
Of the eastern cloud, an hour away;
But forth one wavelet, then another, curled,
Till the whole sunrise, not to be suppressed,
Rose, reddened, and its seething breast
Flickered in bounds, grew gold, then overflowed the world.

Pippa Passes was an early poem, but his painter's hand did not lose its skill. In one of his last, 'Gerard de Lairesse', in *Parleyings with Certain People*, he describes a thunderstorm. Then follows this picture of nature recovering:

But morning's laugh sets all the crags alight
Above the baffled tempest: tree and tree
Stir themselves from the stupor of the night
And every strangled branch resumes its right
To breathe, shakes loose dark's clinging dregs, waves free
In dripping glory. Prone the runnels plunge,
While earth, distent with moisture like a sponge,
Smokes up, and leaves each plant its gem to see,
Each grass-blade's glory-glitter. Had I known
The torrent now turned river?—masterful
Making its rush o'er tumbled ravage—stone
And stub which barred the froths and foams: no bull
Ever broke bounds in formidable sport
More overwhelmingly, till lo, the spasm
Sets him to dare that last mad leap: report
Who may—his fortunes in the deathly chasm
That swallows him in silence!

One might go on to quote the description of the double lunar rainbow in *Christmas Eve*, or that other thunderstorm in *Pippa*

Passes, where the lightning flashes seem to the guilty conscience of Ottima like the probing fingers of the wrath of God. Browning has few rivals as an artist with words. Such a book as this, which deliberately focuses attention on the ethical and religious aspects of his writing, may easily mislead. It leaves largely untouched lyrics as light-hearted as they are lovely, and whole realms of love, joy and fun, as well as of poignant sorrow. Browning was not always moralizing.

Mr D. C. Somervell has an admirable paper on 'The Reputation of Robert Browning'.[1] He ends his wise and witty remarks by speculating on what posterity will think of Browning and also on what it may think of his own generation. He is writing in 1929. 'We shall be noted, perhaps, for the admirable abundance of our good prose, for the tenuity and artificiality of our poetry, and—among other things—for the strange fact that we could not appreciate Browning.' Now, thirty years later, perhaps some of the New Elizabethans are asking questions about some of the odd attitudes of the Georgians, including their paraded dislike of Robert Browning.

[1] *Essays and Studies of the English Association*, vol. xv.

II

The Life Story

Let one more attest
I have lived, seen God's hand through a life-time, and all was
  for best.

Saul

I

Robert Browning was born on May 7, 1812, in Camberwell, then a village on the edge of London. A contemporary writer described it in 1810 as 'a pleasant retreat for those who have a taste for the country, while their avocations still call them daily to London, as it is only three miles from the city'.[1] Before he was a year old Jane Austen at last got *Pride and Prejudice* into print, after fifteen years of vain attempts to find a publisher. Tennyson, Darwin and Gladstone were three years old, Thackeray and Dickens a few months. Elizabeth Barrett was six. Keats and Carlyle were seven; Shelley and Byron in their twenties; Coleridge, Wordsworth and Scott between forty and fifty years old. Victoria was not to be born until 1819.

His Browning grandfather rose to a high position on the staff of the Bank of England. As his first wife he married the daughter of a plantation owner in the West Indies. His son by this marriage, Robert's father, had strong intellectual interests and artistic leanings: he wanted to go to a university and become an artist. Partly under the influence of his second wife, his father would not hear of it. Instead the young man was sent to the

[1] Quoted in W. H. Griffin and H. C. Minchin, *Life of Robert Browning*.

West Indies to learn to manage the estates of his mother, who had died in his infancy. In disgust with what he saw there of slavery, he threw up his lucrative position and came home to England, where his father angrily insisted upon his entering the Bank also.

Browning's other grandfather, on his mother's side, was a German, settled in Dundee where he married a Scot. Their daughter, Robert's mother, was described by Carlyle as 'the true type of Scottish gentlewoman'. When he became famous many fanciful genealogies were provided for him. From the fact that his grandmother was born in the West Indies and his own dark complexion, it was deduced that he had negro blood in him. Because he was very interested in Judaism and wrote several poems about Jews, he was credited with being partly a Jew himself. There is no evidence for either of these guesses and much reason for scepticism. All that is sure about his remoter ancestry is that his paternal grandfather's people came from the West of England.

His parents were members of the York Street Congregational Church, Walworth, and both taught in the Sunday School. A deep life-long affection bound Robert and his father and mother. From her he acquired his love of music: from his father, a man of wide culture, a love of books and of art. There is an attractive picture of his childhood in the poem *Development*, which tells how his father answered his question at the age of five, 'What is a siege and what is Troy?'

He is said to have been a handsome, energetic child, with a keen mind and a fiery temper. He was 'passionately religious' in his boyhood but disliked the unimaginative preaching of his minister. Until he was fourteen he went to a local private school. After that he was educated at home by his father and a succession of tutors. He read voraciously in his father's large collection of books, and the neighbouring Dulwich Art Gallery, with its

THE LIFE STORY

many fine paintings, was a favourite haunt.[1] In addition to the normal literary subjects, he studied music with one of the leading teachers of the day, as well as dancing, riding, boxing, and fencing. For a short time he attended the newly opened University College in Gower Street, to which his father was one of the foundation subscribers, especially the Greek class. Even if he had wished to go, Oxford and Cambridge were closed to nonconformists until 1871. 'Italy was my university,' he used to say. William Sharp records that he was present when in later years someone remarked to Browning, expecting his cordial agreement, that nowadays there was no romance left except in Italy. He replied with a smile: 'Well, I should like to include Camberwell!'[2]

He had the normal 'growing pains' of an able youth and went through a period of rebellion against his parents' beliefs, indulging in a transient fit of vegetarianism and atheism, under the influence of Shelley. This did not last long. Years later, in his preface to *Letters of Shelley*,[3] Browning wrote significantly that men ought not to 'persist in confounding, any more than God confounds, with genuine infidelity and an atheism of the heart those passionate, impatient struggles of a boy towards truth and love . . . Crude convictions of boyhood, conveyed in imperfect and inept forms of speech—for such things all boys have been pardoned'.

Remembering his own frustrated ambitions and the harsh attitude of his own father, Robert's father actively and eagerly encouraged his wish to become a poet. There were various halfhearted attempts to find a job, but in the end he remained at home, studying and writing, supported by his father, until he

---

[1] Founded in 1814, twenty-four years before the National Gallery, it was the chief picture gallery in the country in the opening years of the century.
[2] *Robert Browning*, p. 104.   [3] See p. 14 above.

27

married. One cannot help wondering whether so long a stay under the parental roof, with the ready acceptance of matriarchal control, was really right. It probably accounts for the lack of initiative in practical affairs which hampered him in after life, though he appears to have been business-like in dealing with his publishers. When his mother died he not only mourned her deeply, as was natural, but was actually nervously prostrated for months, much to his wife's distress and concern. When his father died in his eighty-fifth year Browning described him as 'a good, kind-hearted, religious man, whose powers, natural and acquired, would so easily have made him a notable man, had he known what vanity or ambition or the love of money or social influence meant'. They were an affectionate family, father, mother, son and daughter. When the father died, the sister, who had cared for him, came to keep house for Robert, by then a widower.

2

Before he was twenty his poem *Pauline* was published anonymously at the expense of an aunt. It shows great promise, but Browning was very reluctant to include it in his *Collected Works* in 1867, and only did so to prevent unauthorized editions. In the winter of 1833-4 he spent three months in Russia, nominally on the staff of the Russian Consul-general in London. Memories of this visit appear in his poems. He was not yet twenty-three when *Paracelsus* appeared, an extraordinary achievement for anyone, especially one of his age, but it went almost unnoticed, though it led to the formation of friendships that came to mean much, with Dickens, Landor, Carlyle, and with the less known W. J. Fox, the Unitarian preacher and editor, who gave young Browning invaluable help of many kinds. Almost alone among the leading critics, John Forster welcomed the poem and predicted a great future for its writer: 'Without the slightest

THE LIFE STORY

hesitation we name Mr Robert Browning at once with Shelley, Coleridge, Wordsworth.' We shall look more closely later at this poem. In 1837 came *Strafford,* the first of his stage plays, and in 1840 the enigmatic *Sordello,* about which something has been said already. To give a complete list of his numerous books would be tedious and quite beyond the scope of this volume. So far he had attracted little attention, mostly tepid reviews and an uncertain reception in the theatre.

3

It was a prophetic event for Browning when in 1838 he first visited Italy, which was to be his home for many years and his second adopted fatherland. But supreme in importance for the development of his genius and for his life-story was 1844. In that year John Kenyon, a wealthy lover of literature, a schoolfellow and friend of Robert's father, sent his sister, Sarianna, two new volumes of poems by his young 'cousin',[1] Elizabeth Barrett. Browning himself was delighted with them and greatly pleased by a reference to his own poetry which coupled his name with those of Wordsworth and Tennyson.

Elizabeth Barrett, now thirty-eight, had received considerable acclaim as a poet and was a frequent contributor to literary journals. A woman of wide knowledge and a classical scholar, she had also translated into verse works by several of the Greek dramatists. But physically she was a sad wreck of a woman. A serious illness following an accident had led to her being moved to Torquay in 1838. She begged that her eldest brother, to whom she was bound by closer ties of affection than to any one

---

[1] According to Elizabeth, this was 'a courtesy title': he was apparently a second cousin. Kenyon seems to have been a delightful and widely loved person, who knew everybody in the literary world. He did more for Elizabeth than anyone except Robert. See G. B. Taplin, *Life of Elizabeth Barrett Browning.*

else, should stay there with her. When he was drowned in a boating accident in July 1840, Elizabeth blamed herself since it was for her sake that he was in Torquay at all. The shock nearly destroyed her reason and for months her life seemed to hang by a thread. The tragedy haunted her all her days.

When well enough she was moved by slow stages in a kind of ambulance to the family home in Wimpole Street in London. For five years she scarcely ever left her room, which was sealed against draughts from within and fresh air from without, and came to have a morbid love for its shelter, dark, silent and airless. She refused to see more than a handful of friends and the smallest change in her dull routine brought on headaches and insomnia. It was to this Elizabeth that Robert, approaching his thirty-third birthday, wrote in January 1845, expressing profound admiration for her poems and asking if he might call. She hesitated and they corresponded for five months before she agreed to see him. The letters revealed that they had much in common, devotion to poetry, religious convictions, wide interests, liberal and humanitarian sympathies. When they met, the exuberantly healthy Robert saw lying on a sofa a little woman with large, impressive eyes and a pale face framed in ringlets. Before they met at all she had classed him among the great poets of the day. She had a portrait of him on her wall, beside those of Tennyson and Wordsworth. On his part he never had any doubt to the day of his death that her poetry was superior to his own. 'She has genius,' he remarked in 1866, 'I am only a painstaking fellow. The true creative power is hers, not mine.'

They continued to meet and correspond as fellow poets, comparing notes on craftsmanship and exchanging drafts of poems. Three months after the first meeting Elizabeth wrote to him: 'It is quite startling and humiliating to observe how you combine

THE LIFE STORY

such large tracts of experience of outer and inner life, of books and men, of the world and the arts of it, curious knowledge as well as general knowledge . . . and deep thinking as well as wide acquisitions.'[1] The friendship rapidly matured. Soon they passed beyond poetry to more personal matters and Robert learned with incredulity the state of affairs in the Barrett household. Her father ruled with what seemed to him an unchallengeable divine right. He could be kind and affectionate and jolly, and Elizabeth was very fond of him: he had many admirable qualities. But he was dictatorial and peremptory and demanded unquestioning obedience, even from a daughter as old as Elizabeth, as he had done from his wife when she was alive.[2] He was in the habit of taking decisions that affected the whole family, such as moving their home from one part of England to another, without consultation or explanation. He had a pathological aversion from the thought of any of his daughters getting married. It was a dreadful situation.

But month by month, with a new joy and interest in life, Elizabeth's health improved. Step by step she became capable of actions which both she and her friends had thought impossible. At last her father refused to countenance a stay abroad which was strongly urged by her doctors. She could only go to Italy, he said, after much discussion, 'under his heaviest displeasure'. The dispute caused an estrangement between them which made her ready to yield at last to Robert's pleadings that she would leave home and marry him. 'Do decide, Ba,'[3] he kept on urging, while she kept finding reasons for procrastination, though at the same time protesting that she was his to command. She was tortured by the inner conflict.

---

[1] August 20, 1845. *Letters of Robert Browning and Elizabeth Barrett Browning*, vol. i, pp. 168f.
[2] She died when Elizabeth was twenty-two.
[3] Elizabeth's pet name, first bestowed by her brother Edward.

4

At last Elizabeth summoned up courage to defy her father. On September 12, 1846, accompanied only by her maid, she drove to Marylebone Church, the nearest to her home, and they were married. She returned home at once, but a week later, with her dog and her maid, she crept out of the house while the family were at dinner. Eventually they reached Italy, where for the fifteen years of their wedded life they made their home.

It is a wonder that they carried through their complicated adventure and got across the Channel at all, in view of Robert's repeated muddles over such sordid details as the times of trains and boats. Luckily, once in Paris, they were able to seek out an old friend, Mrs Jameson. Startled at seeing them though delighted at their marriage, which they had had to keep secret from everyone, she saw that Elizabeth, though obviously happy, was nervous and greatly agitated. She took them under her wing and convoyed them the rest of the way to Italy. She wrote to a friend at the time that Robert was 'in all the common things of this life the most unpractical of men, and the most uncalculating, rash—in short, the worst *manager* I ever met with'.[1]

Elizabeth received a bitter letter from her father, saying that he had disinherited her and for the rest of his life would consider her as dead. He kept his word. Her letters remained unanswered: indeed, a bundle of them was later returned, unopened, under cover of a violent letter addressed to Robert. Only once did he reply. Six years after the marriage in 1852, when they were paying a brief visit to London, Elizabeth wrote to her father begging to be allowed to see him. His brutal answer, with 'the plain intention of giving me as much pain as possible', ordered her not to annoy him with any more letters. Another

[1] To Lady Byron, quoted in Miller, *Robert Browning*, p. 133.

daughter, Henrietta, whose request for consent to her marriage was described by him as an 'insult', likewise fled from home to be married and also became an outcast.[1]

Robert and Elizabeth had no occasion to write each other any more letters, for they were never separated for more than a day. Though they moved about, they made their home in Florence. Her health showed an astonishing improvement. She went for long walks and donkey rides, climbed hills, and travelled around, to the amazement of her friends. On March 9, 1849, to their great rejoicing, Elizabeth, now forty-three, after three miscarriages, bore a son, Robert Barrett Browning, known in the family as 'Pen'. It was an ideally happy marriage and a partnership in great poetic writing, each inspiring the other, though they worked apart, not showing a poem until it was completed. Of course, being human, they had differences of opinion—about Louis Napoleon, spiritualism, and the right way of bringing up children, including Pen. But these were on the surface and did not disturb the deep flow of mutual love; though one or two recent writers have suggested otherwise. To the very end Elizabeth kept on referring in letters to her sisters and intimate friends to his constant love and care for his invalid wife: 'Husband, lover, nurse—not one of these has Robert been to me, but all three together.'

Their love as Elizabeth saw it is commemorated in the so-called *Sonnets from the Portuguese,* a title suggested by one of her earlier poems, which she put into his hands in manuscript two years after their marriage. It tells us much about him that he should have called out such wonderful love-poetry. His response may be read in *One Word More,* appended to his *Men and Women,* and in the invocation of *The Ring and the Book.* It is reflected also in *By the Fireside,* their love story in disguise.

[1] The story is told at length in Taplin's *Life*.

THE FAITH OF ROBERT BROWNING

In *One Word More* he says that every artist wishes to do something out of his usual medium to please the woman he loves. Rafael wrote sonnets, while Dante began to paint a picture. He himself could not write music, paint a picture, or carve a statue; he could only write this poem, though in a metre to be used only this once. Now he speaks for himself, not as one of his imagined men and women in the rest of the volume. If, he says, the moon fell in love with a mortal she would turn to him the other unseen side.

> What were seen? None knows, none ever shall know.
> Only this is sure—the sight were other,
> Not the moon's same side, born late in Florence,
> Dying now impoverished here in London.
> God be thanked, the meanest of his creatures
> Boasts two soul-sides, one to face the world with,
> One to show a woman when he loves her!
>
> This I say of me, but think of you, Love!
> This to you—yourself my moon of poets!
> Ah, but that's the world's side, there's the wonder,
> Thus they see you, praise you, think they know you!
> There, in turn I stand with them and praise you—
> Out of my own self, I dare to phrase it.
> But the best is when I glide from out them,
> Cross a step or two of dubious twilight,
> Come out on the other side, the novel
> Silent silver lights and darks undreamed of,
> Where I hush and bless myself with silence.

'It requires a poet of consummate genius, like Browning,' wrote William Temple, referring to this poem 'to reveal the beauty of the deep peaceful happiness of married love'.[1]

---

[1] *Essays in Christian Politics*, p. 117.

THE LIFE STORY

5

They lived at first on very straitened means, though they found that living was much cheaper than in England; poetry, especially Robert's, not being very remunerative. But she had a small private income of her own, from an uncle's legacy, and Kenyon, her 'fairy godfather' as she called him, made them an allowance of £100 a year after the birth of Pen. At his death in 1856 his generous legacies to them both removed all anxiety. Mr Barrett did not mention Elizabeth in his will.

It is interesting to read the account in his journal of a visit paid to them in the spring of 1858 by Nathaniel Hawthorne, the American novelist. Browning was young and handsome and in vigorous health, 'a most vivid and quick thoughted person'. 'His nonsense is of very genuine and excellent quality, the true bubble and effervescence of a bright and powerful mind . . . She looked elfin rather than earthly; her black ringlets cluster into her neck and make her face look whiter by their sable perfection.' Mrs Hawthorne noticed something more, the 'deep pain furrowed into her face—such pain that the great happiness of her life cannot smooth it away'. Browning is described by others also at this time as a handsome man of striking appearance, with dark brown, wavy hair, worn longer than is now customary, quick-witted, alert, with a clear, pleasant and resonant voice. Tennyson's elder brother Frederick, who lived in Florence, became a close friend and described Browning as 'a man of infinite learning, jest and bonhommie, and moreover a sterling heart that reverbs no hollowness'.

Browning had a considerable knowledge and love of painting, music and sculpture, evident in many of his poems, which residence in Italy gave them opportunity to cultivate. With 'enormous superfluity of vital energy', in Elizabeth's words, when he laid aside poetry-writing he would go for long walks, spend hours at the piano at which he was a talented amateur, or absorb himself in drawing or modelling in clay. Highly strung, with a rather excitable temperament, he was capable of sudden outbursts of rage, 'thunderstorms' his friend Gosse called them, directed against literary critics, especially if they did not appreciate Elizabeth's poems, spiritualistic mediums, politicians, and people who volunteered to write biographies of his wife.

In a few years the fundamental weaknesses of her constitution reasserted themselves and she again became a good deal of an invalid. She died suddenly and quite unexpectedly of lung trouble in June 1861. She was buried in Florence.

6

After the funeral Robert left Florence, never to return. He went back to London and devoted himself to the care and education of their son and his eventual training as an artist. The unutterable dreariness of life without Elizabeth was underlined by the prosaic ugliness of the Paddington neighbourhood contrasted with the sunshine and colour of Italy. He said himself that his life was 'as grey as the London sky'. At first he lived the life of a recluse and it was long before he regained courage to go about again. When he did emerge he did it thoroughly. He would work steadily in the mornings and then seek relief in all sorts of exhibitions, dinner parties and the like. He is said not to have missed an important concert for years.

It may be recorded here that the son caused considerable trouble and anxiety to his father and aunt. He was lazy and unco-operative, yet one cannot help feeling somewhat sorry for him. Elizabeth certainly 'spoiled' him, in the full sense of the word, and he carried on into adult life the complete absence of self-discipline allowed in childhood by his doting mother. After her death, which in itself must have destroyed his foundations,

THE LIFE STORY

he found himself removed to a strange cold land from the Italy where he belonged and whose language he spoke for preference. His father's first act, meant in all kindness, was to cut off his long golden ringlets and to replace the curious garments of velvets and satins in which his mother clothed him up to the age of twelve, by the sober clothing of an ordinary English schoolboy.[1] No wonder he found it difficult to adjust himself. He had not been allowed to go to school by his mother and even in England he continued to be taught rather unsystematically at home. He failed to pass the entrance examination for Balliol College, Oxford, and when he got into Christ Church he was sent down after about a year for failing to work. He eventually emerged as an artist of some talent but given to the production of enormous canvases, few of which sold. Until the age of thirty-eight he had to be considerably subsidized by his father, when he married a wealthy American wife, from whom he was soon separated. There were no children.

As we have seen, Browning had to go through a long period of neglect before his work achieved any wide recognition. He felt some bitterness about it, and when after he had become established certain critics said that they at least had always recognized his genius, he would remark sourly that if they had said so in public ten or twenty years earlier it would have been a real help. In contrast, Elizabeth's books went through edition after edition. When Wordsworth died in 1850, it was she who was suggested as a possible successor to the poet laureateship, which was eventually given to Tennyson. *Aurora Leigh* especially brought her great fame. It is a very long novel in verse, full of impossible people and incredible events and was coldly received by the reviewers, but it exactly met the popular taste of the day. It

---

[1] Described in a long letter to his sister soon after Elizabeth's death. *New Letters*, pp. 131ff.

soon reached a fifth edition, while Robert's books barely paid their way. The disparity in recognition worried both of them, though he never wavered in his profound admiration for her work and rejoiced in its success. He was so discouraged for a time that he gave up poetry and devoted himself to modelling. But soon after his return to London the position began to change. He was invited to become editor of the *Cornhill* magazine, a volume of 'Selections' from his poetry appeared in 1863, and in the same year his publishers issued a collected edition of his works. After the appearance of *The Ring and the Book* in 1868 he became famous, and readers went back to his comparatively neglected earlier poems, though for long his popularity in America was greater than in England. In 1868 a six volume edition of his poems was issued. He still had twenty years of active life before him.

7

Many honours came to him. He was given honorary degrees by Oxford, Edinburgh and Cambridge, and was made an Honorary Fellow of Balliol. The distinguished Benjamin Jowett, Master of Balliol, had a great admiration for Browning the man, though only a qualified respect for his poetry. It is interesting to read his verdict. After meeting Browning for the first time in 1865 he wrote that though he felt he was getting too old to make new friends he had just made one. 'It is impossible to speak without enthusiasm of his (Browning's) open, generous nature and his great ability and knowledge. I had no idea that there was a perfectly sensible poet in the world, entirely free from vanity, jealousy or any other littleness, and thinking no more of himself than any ordinary man. His great energy is very remarkable and his determination to make the most of the remainder of his life.'[1]

[1] Abbott and Campbell, *Life of Benjamin Jowett*, vol. i, pp. 400-1.

THE LIFE STORY

A testimony to his standing with students is seen in the repeated invitations to accept nomination as Lord Rector of Scottish universities, which he declined. A Browning Society was formed which he regarded with a kind of cautious benevolence, deprecating the undue solemnity with which they analysed his poems and the rather silly adulation in which some of its members indulged. He continued to write throughout his life and his last volume *Asolando*, was published on the day of his death. As he lay dying in Venice he heard with pleasure of the eager advance demand.

Opinions differ about his later work. Mrs Miller, in her interesting and often illuminating psychological study,[1] will have it that in his later years Browning was a changed man. She speaks of 'the extinction of genius' and thinks that all that was left of him was the 'bourgeois', in Henry James' word, who went to dinner parties. Here as elsewhere she seems to me too sweeping in her judgments, just as at other points she makes deductions that go well beyond the evidence. It is certainly wrong to dismiss everything written after 1868, as some do, though he never again reached the heights of *The Ring and the Book*. *Ferishtah's Fancies*, 1884, and *Parleyings*, 1887, which Mrs Miller brushes away as totally unworthy, contain many memorable passages, though on the whole they are more argumentation than poetry and parts of them read like the work of a tired old man. *Asolando*, 1889, the last book of all, shows a remarkable recovery of power.

In the autumn of 1878, after seventeen years absence, Browning revisited Italy. He did not go to Florence but to his beloved Asolo, the home of his Pippa, which gave the title to his last volume, and to Venice, where he spent some time each autumn for the next three years. In 1889, at the age of seventy-eight, a

[1] *Robert Browning: A Portrait*.

friend invited him to stay at Asolo again. From there in the autumn he went to Venice to join his son and daughter-in-law. A chill led to heart failure and death on December 12, 1889.

Burial in Westminster Abbey was offered, and on the last day of the year, in a London shrouded in dim, yellow fog, he found his rightful place in Poets' Corner. A similar offer was then made for Elizabeth's remains, but the removal of the body from Florence would have been against the wishes of the people of that city, as well as of Robert himself, and the offer was declined.

III

The Eternal Purpose[1]

> What were life
> Did soul stand still therein, forego her strife
> Through the ambiguous Present to the goal
> Of some all-reconciling Future
>
> *Parleyings*

> Life with all it holds of joy or woe
> Is just our chance of the prize of learning love.
>
> *A Death in the Desert*

Browning wrote no religious or devotional verse like that of George Herbert or Keble. He composed no hymns. Many of his poems have no obvious connection with religion at all. Yet his work as a whole, and outcrops within it in the most unexpected places, is shot through with deep veins of religious feeling and thought. It is unmistakably the work of a profoundly religious man. In several poems, such as *Christmas Eve and Easter Day*, *La Saisiaz*, and *Ferishtah's Fancies*, he addresses himself to religious issues in his own person, as it were, as he does in the name of others in *The Ring and the Book*, *A Death in the Desert*, *An Epistle of Karshish* and *Saul*.

I

What was Browning's attitude to the Christian Faith? The

[1] The title of this chapter is taken from the Epistle to the Ephesians. It seems to me that Browning's religious teaching is an admirable commentary on Ephesians 3.11-19.

question has been much debated. William Temple, who referred to Browning as his 'favourite poet' in his presidential address to the English Association in 1939, declared at another time that 'the three continuously formative influences on his mind were Plato, St John, and Robert Browning'.[1] 'Browning's genius,' wrote Temple, 'is fundamentally and thoroughly Christian: to Browning the climax of history, the crown of philosophy and the consummation of poetry is unquestionably the Incarnation.'[2]

On the other hand, Lascelles Abercrombie has no use for Browning when he talks about religion and thinks his views on it quite unimportant. 'It was not for him to judge life but simply to portray it.' 'We can see now that Browning was not a poet whose mission could ever have been the interpretation or even the valuing of life. The poems in which he attempted such a business are the mere aberrations of his genius. There are not very many of them: in the whole mass of his work their bulk is comparatively small, and they should not be allowed to distract our attention from his success, much less trouble our admiration for it.'[3] This is a very odd judgment and it is not surprising to discover that Mr Abercrombie thinks *La Saisiaz* and *Christmas Eve* poor stuff: 'The thought is a doggerel rendering of abysmally dull sectarian theology, futile, small and profitless, which can never, one would think, have had much importance and now has none whatever.'[4] This reminds one of the title of a once famous essay by John Foster (1823) on 'The Aversion of Men of Taste to Evangelical Religion'.

Mr J. M. Cohen, a better judge, also thinks that *Christmas Eve* and *Easter Day* 'as a whole are a failure' and 'founded the awk-

[1] Prof. Dorothy Emmet in Iremonger's *Life of William Temple*, p. 527.
[2] *Op. cit.*, p. 46.
[3] *The Great Victorians*, ed. H. J. and Hugh Massingham, p. 91.
[4] *Op. cit.*, p. 90.

ward legend of Browning's message'.[1] And one or two books about him repeat a story that he once replied 'No' to the direct question whether he was a Christian. The story needs corroboration. It contradicts numerous declarations the other way. In any case it all depends on what you mean by 'Christian'. We are not told the context of the question, asuming the story to be accurate. In some senses of the word, the rigid, sectarian, fundamentalist, verbal inspirationist senses, he would certainly have said 'No'. In a letter of August 15, 1846, Elizabeth wrote to Robert that she felt unwilling 'to put on any of the liveries of the sects'. She 'could pray anywhere and with all sorts of worshippers', but she liked 'beyond comparison best, the simplicity of the Dissenters . . . and the principle of a church as they hold it, I hold it too'. She was not attracted either by the ritualists or the unitarians. In reply Robert declared that he responded to these views with his whole soul: these were his own convictions.

Mrs Sutherland Orr, a close friend of his later years, gives the impression in her *Life of Browning* of wishing to minimize his Christian attachments and to make him out as deeply religious indeed, but as holding a rather ethereal type of vague theism, apparently after her own heart. This is not only at variance with Browning's own writings and practice but is contradicted by the testimony of other friends and of his wife. It is, indeed, in contradiction to much evidence scattered throughout Mrs Orr's own *Life*. She declares at one point that as soon as he grew up he left off regular church attendance. This seems nonsense. Before his marriage it was a family joke that Robert was always going off to hear some new preacher, 'to pastors new'. During their stay in Paris in the winter of 1851–2 Elizabeth wrote: 'Robert keeps steady to the little church of French Independents, where he

[1] *Robert Browning*, p. 176.

THE FAITH OF ROBERT BROWNING

"quite loves" that "angelic M. Bridel, who has the face of Tennyson and the apostle John", he says, "together".[1] Similarly in November 1854 she writes to a friend that Robert went off punctually every Sunday to the Presbyterian church in Florence, though the minister, she thought, was a very dull preacher. When the minister died, Robert was one of the chief mourners at the funeral. We are told by Mrs Orr herself that he never failed to attend chapel when he visited Oxford or Cambridge, and that he went regularly when staying in the country. There is a tablet in the parish church at Llantysilio to mark his frequent attendance when living at Llangollen with his sister. In Venice he regularly attended the services at a Waldensian chapel, and at the Reformed church in Normandy when he stayed with his friend Milsand. After his wife's death, when he was again in London, he became a 'seat-holder' in Bedford Congregational Chapel, and in 1884 wrote an introduction to a volume of sermons by the minister, the Rev. Thomas Jones. We are told that he often went to services in Westminster Abbey, and that he had many friends among parsons and liked to discuss religion with them. So he does not seem to have given up church going with any great consistency or determination. If I seem to have laboured this point, it is to counter the wild statements sometimes made about his habits.

Mrs Orr was perhaps in not unnatural revolt against the practice of too readily claiming him as a Free Church prophet and of publishing books about his Christian message, with indiscriminate quotations. Browning was not a systematic theologian, though he wrote better theology than some of the professionals. He probably thought himself unorthodox. He did not believe in 'eternal punishment' and may have thought, erron-

---

[1] Betty Miller, *Robert Browning: A Portrait*, p. 162.

eously, that it was a Christian doctrine.[1] Judging from several poems, he found difficulty in accepting the literal historicity of some parts of the Gospel story. But many Christian scholars hesitate as to where to draw the precise line between historical event and interpretative comment, especially in the Fourth Gospel. It is not clear that Browning went further than this, and the insights of modern New Testament scholarship would have helped him here. He lived in an era of 'take it or leave it'. But he revolted from the sweeping destructiveness of some of the then current German criticism which sought to dissolve the figure of Jesus into a myth. As is shown by his practice and his writing, he felt most at home in Free Church circles, though he rebelled against the ugliness and crudity associated with some aspects of contemporary Dissent. Certainly he had not found a home for his spirit in the Independent chapel where he had been brought up. His wife once described him as 'descended from the blood of all the Puritans and educated by the strictest of dissenters'. He remained a Puritan in much, but it was a puritanism modified as with many seventeenth-century Puritans such as Colonel Hutchinson, by keen artistic sympathies, and by a searching mind and far-reaching intellectual curiosity, like that of Richard Baxter. He was not an ascetic, in the sense of one who despises the pleasures and beauties of the world, but he was one in the more technical sense of moral discipline. For him, as for the original Puritans, life was a school or a battle field.

It is noteworthy that Dean Inge counted Wordsworth and Browning among the Christian mystics. He lays particular stress on Browning's belief that 'the friction of active life and especially the experience of human love are necessary to realize the Divine

---

[1] *Ixion*, a difficult poem, is a protest against the belief, as is *A Camel Driver* in *Ferishtah's Fancies*. F. D. Maurice was dismissed from his post as Professor of Theology in King's College, London, in 1853, for attacking the doctrine.

in man'. 'He who "finds love full in his nature" cannot doubt that in this, as in all else, the Creator must far surpass the creature.'[1] In knowing love we know God. Inge also refers to Browning's frequent use of Eckhart's image, whether consciously quoted or not, of the spark in the soul; as in this from *Any Wife to Any Husband*:

> It would not be because my eye grew dim
> Thou couldst not find the love there, thanks to Him
>   Who never is dishonoured in the spark
> He gave us from his fire of fires, and bade
> Remember whence it sprang, nor be afraid
>   While that burns on, though all the rest grow dark.[2]

2

We shall try now to get to closer quarters with his specifically religious teaching, trying all the time not to forget the danger of attributing to the author the views of his characters.

Fundamental is his belief that human life has meaning, because of the plan and purpose of the Creator. Though 'the little mind of man' cannot fully grasp that plan and purpose, we can in part and we can willingly co-operate with it. Nature and man together are manifestations of God's self-revealing activities, crowned in Christ. So the Pope prays:

> O Thou,—as represented here to me
> In such conception as my soul allows,—
> Under Thy measureless, my atom width!—
> Man's mind, what is it but a convex glass
> Wherein are gathered all the scattered points
> Picked out of the immensity of sky,
> To re-unite there, be our heaven for earth,
> Our known unknown, our God revealed to man?
> Existent somewhere, somehow, as a whole;
> Here, as a whole proportioned to our sense,—

[1] *Christian Mysticism*, p. 318.
[2] See also p. 93.

> There, (which is nowhere, speech must babble thus!)
> In the absolute immensity, the whole
> Appreciable solely by Thyself,—
> Here, by the little mind of man, reduced
> To littleness that suits his faculty.

From the study of nature and of himself man can learn much, can

> Conjecture of the worker by the work:
> Is there strength there?—enough: intelligence?
> Ample: but goodness in a like degree?
> Not to the human eye in the present state.

The needed completion of the divine revelation is given in the story of Jesus.

> What lacks, then, of perfection fit for God
> But just the instance which this tale supplies
> Of love without a limit? So is strength,
> So is intelligence; let love be so,
> Unlimited in its self-sacrifice,
> Then is the tale true and God shows complete.

Such a belief was not easily held. Browning's generation was a time of great intellectual unrest. No one can begin to understand the Victorian age who does not recognize the seismic upheavals of doubt cracking the surface of complacency. The repeal of the Corn Laws, the Reform Bill, the coming of popular education and the progressive extension of the franchise, were its political expression. At the same time the advances of science and the theory of evolution seemed to threaten the foundations of religious belief. Geology, astronomy and biology were discrediting the biblical pictures of the age of the earth and its place in the universe, and of the origins of mankind. Astronomy saw the world evolving out of a nebula, not coming into being by an act of creation, and evolution appeared to place man *much* lower

THE FAITH OF ROBERT BROWNING

than the angels. Huxley, Spencer and Tyndal were asserting that science was the only reliable road to knowledge and that since it did not lead to God, we could know nothing for certain about him: agnosticism was the only proper attitude for modern man.

Christianity was under attack from another quarter too. Strauss's *Leben Jesus*, published in 1835 and translated into English by George Eliot in 1846, declared that while we could still find noble spiritual truths in the Gospel story its historicity was open to serious question. From a somewhat different standpoint, though equally disturbing, Renan's *Vie de Jesus* appeared in English in 1863, seeking to dissolve the accretions of legend which had gathered round the figure of the simple Galilean teacher. The appearance of *Essays and Reviews* in 1860 was another cause of storm and distress among Christians generally. Written by a group of Anglicans the volume not only challenged many widely held beliefs but did so in what seemed a deliberately provocative manner. Browning's familiarity with all these challenges to faith is made evident again and again in his poems and they are often explicitly discussed. We know from his letters too that he had read the literature at first hand.

3

For himself he found no difficulty for his faith in the doctrine of evolution, though many in his generation did. 'The young poet had even grasped what took the world another half century to perceive, that the idea of evolution levelled upwards and not downwards, spiritualized nature rather than naturalized spirit.'[1] He frequently traces the divine activity in the whole evolu-

---

[1] Henry Jones, *Cambridge History of English Literature*, vol. xiii. 2, p. 57. It is somewhat startling to realize that Browning's *Paracelsus*, 1835, like Tennyson's *In Memoriam*, 1850, was published long before Darwin's *The Origin of Species*, 1859, which systematized and developed with epoch-making force scientific theories already widely current.

THE ETERNAL PURPOSE

tionary process from the beginning up to man and in human experience. Here, for example, is Prince Hohenstiel Schwangau, no alias for Browning but speaking for him in this:

> 'Will you have why and wherefore, and the fact
> Made plain as pikestaff?' modern Science asks.
> 'That mass man sprung from was a jelly-lump
> Once on a time; he kept an after course
> Through fish and insect, reptile, bird and beast,
> Till he attained to be an ape at last
> Or last but one. And if this doctrine shock
> In aught the natural pride'. . . Friend, banish fear,
> The natural humility replies!
>
> . . . .
>
>   God takes time.
> I like the thought He should have lodged me once
> I' the hole, the cave, the hut, the tenement,
> The mansion and the palace; made me learn
> The feel o' the first, before I found myself
> Loftier i' the last.

There is a wonderful picture in *Paracelsus* of God's joy in his developing creative purpose:

> The centre-fire heaves underneath the earth,
> And the earth changes like a human face;
> The molten ore bursts up among the rocks,
> Winds into the stone's heart, outbranches bright
> In hidden mines, spots barren river-beds,
> Crumbles into fine sand where sunbeams bask—
> God joys therein. The wroth sea's waves are edged
> With foam, white as the bitten lip of hate,
> When, in the solitary waste, strange groups
> Of young volcanos come up, cyclops-like,
> Staring together with their eyes on flame—
> God tastes a pleasure in their uncouth pride.
> Then all is still; earth is a wintry clod:
> But spring-wind, like a dancing psaltress, passes

Over its breast to waken it, rare verdure
Buds tenderly upon rough banks, between
The withered tree-roots and the cracks of frost,
Like a smile striving with a wrinkled face;
The grass grows bright, the boughs are swoln with blooms
Like chrysalids impatient for the air,
The shining dorrs are busy, beetles run
Along the furrows, ants make their ado;
Above, birds fly in merry flocks, the lark
Soars up and up, shivering for very joy;
Afar the ocean sleeps; white fishing-gulls
Flit where the strand is purple with its tribe
Of nested limpets; savage creatures seek
Their loves in wood and plain—and God renews
His ancient rapture. Thus he dwells in all,
From life's minute beginnings, up at last
To man—the consummation of this scheme
Of being,

. . . .

For these things tend still upward, progress is
The law of life, man is not Man as yet.
. . . All tended to mankind,
And, man produced, all has its end thus far:
But in completed man begins anew
A tendency to God.

4

It is in order that man may become Man that he is placed here. Browning agreed with Keats that this earth is no 'vale of tears' but rather 'a vale of soul-making'. In the revealing dedication of *Sordello* he declares that its 'historical decoration was purposely of no more importance than a background requires; my stress lay on the incidents in the development of a soul: little else is worth study. I, at least, always thought so'. Human life, Browning says repeatedly, is meant to be a training school for the growth of character.

THE ETERNAL PURPOSE

> What were life
> Did soul stand still therein, forego her strife
> Through the ambiguous Present to the goal
> Of some all-reconciling Future?[1]

This is an essential postulate of a reasonable life, he asserts in *La Saisiaz*.

> I have lived, then, done and suffered, loved and hated, learnt and taught
> This—there is no reconciling wisdom with a world distraught,
> Goodness with triumphant evil, power with failure in the aim,
> If—(to my own sense, remember! though none other feel the same!)—
> If you bar me from assuming earth to be a pupil's place,
> And life, time,—with all their chances, changes,—just probation-space,
> Mine, for me.

This does not mean that life must always be a grim business. Nor did it mean that Browning despised the physical and wanted man always to be solemnly considering his 'latter end'. He knew man was body-soul. A healthy, vigorous man, he enjoyed life to the full.

> How good is man's life, the mere living! how fit to employ
> All the heart and the soul and the senses for ever in joy,

cries David in *Saul*. And Rabbi ben Ezra advises:

> Let us not always say
> 'Spite of this flesh to-day
> 'I strove, made head, gained ground upon the whole!'
> As the bird wings and sings,
> Let us cry 'All good things
> 'Are ours, nor soul helps flesh more, now, than flesh helps soul!'

---

[1] 'Gerard de Lairesse' in *Parleyings*.

Yet in this process of training, sorrow, pain, even sin, have their parts to play. Life is struggle. The worst fate of all would be 'a ghastly smooth life, dead at heart'. (*Easter Day*). It is because life is a probation and God has a purpose of love for us that He does not leave us alone. A famous passage from *Bishop Blougram's Apology* demands to be quoted here once more. The poem records an after-dinner chat between a Roman Catholic bishop and a rather shallow journalist, a professed unbeliever, Mr Gigadibs, who has made no secret of the fact that he despises the bishop. No man who is not a fool or a knave, he thinks, could be in the bishop's position, with the implied obligation to hold all kinds of unbelievable beliefs. The debate is serious for all its humour and the bishop in his self-defence—that being the sense of 'apology' here—presents the case for belief over against the case for unbelief. He admits that he finds real difficulties in some of the Christian dogmas, but if on that account he were to choose unbelief he would be no better off. In the course of the clever, casuistical argument the bishop says many things which we must now pass over, some ironical and *ad hominem*. For the moment let us note his contention that, to say the least of it, unbelief has its difficulties too and is as hard to defend as belief. If we try to settle down in unbelief,

> Just when we are safest, there's a sunset-touch,
> A fancy from a flower-bell, some one's death,
> A chorus-ending from Euripides,—
> And that's enough for fifty hopes and fears
> As old and new at once as nature's self,
> To rap and knock and enter in our soul,
> Take hands and dance there, a fantastic ring,
> Round the ancient idol, on his base again,—
> The grand Perhaps! We look on helplessly.
> There the old misgivings, crooked questions are!

The same point is put in *Cristina*:

THE ETERNAL PURPOSE

> Oh, we're sunk enough here, God knows!
>   But not quite so sunk that moments,
> Sure tho' seldom, are denied us,
>   When the spirit's true endowments
> Stand out plainly from its false ones,
>   And apprise it if pursuing
> Or the right way or the wrong way,
>   To its triumph or undoing.
>
> There are flashes struck from midnights,
>   There are fire-flames noondays kindle,
> Whereby piled-up honours perish,
>   Whereby swollen ambitions dwindle,
> While just this or that poor impulse,
>   Which for once had play unstifled,
> Seems the sole work of a life-time
>   That away the rest have trifled.

If the world be not a training place provided by divine love the only possible alternative is that it is a scene of capricious cruelty or indifference by 'whatever gods there be', such as Caliban imagines in his god Setebos, who is only amusing himself.

> 'Thinketh, such shows nor right nor wrong in Him,
> Nor kind, nor cruel: He is strong and Lord
> 'Am strong myself compared to yonder crabs
> That march now from the mountain to the sea.
> 'Let twenty pass, and stone the twenty-first,
> Loving not, hating not, just choosing so.
> 'Say, the first straggler that boasts purple spots
> Shall join the file, one pincer twisted off;
> 'Say, this bruised fellow shall receive a worm,
> And two worms he whose nippers end in red;
> As it likes me each time, I do: so He.

As Thomas Hardy put it: 'The President of the Immortals had finished his sport with Tess.' Against such a view Browning's whole being revolted.

THE FAITH OF ROBERT BROWNING

Nevertheless, he admits that life is only intelligible, rational and bearable if there is another life to come. Here at least we may quote *Fifine at the Fair*.

> I search but cannot see
> What purpose serves the soul that strives, or world it tries
> Conclusions with, unless the fruit of victories
> Stay, one and all, stored up and guaranteed its own
> For ever, by some mode whereby shall be made known
> The gain of every life. Death reads the title clear—
> What each soul for itself conquered from out things here:
> Since, in the seeing soul, all worth lies, I assert

In a later chapter we shall look more closely at Browning's beliefs about the future life.

5

The key to the understanding of life, Browning declares, is love, and love is the lesson we are here to learn. The power of God is obvious: His love is not so obvious.

> In youth I looked to these very skies,
> And probing their immensities,
> I found God there, His visible power;
> Yet felt in my heart, amid all its sense
> Of the power, an equal evidence
> That His love, there too, was the nobler dower.
> For the loving worm within its clod,
> Were diviner than a loveless god
> Amid his worlds, I will dare to say.

Yet *Christmas Eve* goes on to show that experience taught him that love was there too.

> So, gazing up, in my youth, at love
> As seen through power, ever above
> All modes which make it manifest,
> My soul brought all to a single test—

> That He, the Eternal First and Last,
> Who, in His power, had so surpassed
> All man conceives of what is might,—
> Whose wisdom, too, showed infinite,
> —Would prove as infinitely good;
> Would never, (my soul understood,)
> With power to work all love desires,
> Bestow e'en less than man requires.

Love, in Browning's creed, is the ultimate truth about God and the last word of religion and morality. The very essence of God is love and the highest purpose of human life is that a man should learn to love. David argues from his love for Saul, his eager unselfish longing to do everything he possibly can to help him in his great need, to the assurance that there must be in the heart of God at least as great a love.[1] So Jesus argued: 'If you then, bad as you are, know how to give your children what is good for them, how much more will your heavenly Father give good things to those who ask him.'[2] As, on the other hand, the New Testament pleads from the evidence in Christ of the love of God to the need for men to show a like love to their fellows, so does Browning, as in *Christmas Eve*:

> Take all in a word: the truth in God's breast
> Lies trace for trace upon ours impressed:
> Though He is so bright and we so dim,
> We are made in his image to witness Him.

Life was devised for that. In *The Ring and the Book* the Pope finds comfort in that faith, in face of the pain and evil in the world:

> I can believe this dread machinery
> Of sin and sorrow, would confound me else.
> Devised,—all pain, at most expenditure
> Of pain by Who devised pain,—to evolve,

[1] See p. 64 below.
[2] Matt. 7.11 (NEB).

> By new machinery in counterpart,
> The moral qualities of man—how else?—
> To make him love in turn and be beloved,
> Creative and self-sacrificing too,
> And thus eventually God-like.

In *A Death in the Desert* John sums it all up, as in his epistles:

> For life, with all it yields of joy and woe,
> And hope and fear,—believe the aged friend,—
> Is just our chance o' the prize of learning love,
> What love hath been, indeed, and is.

6

It is characteristic of Browning to set love and knowledge in antithesis and to proclaim the supremacy of love. This is the theme of *Paracelsus*, a work of remarkable maturity though written when he was twenty-three.[1] Based upon the life of a Swiss scientist and philosopher of the sixteenth century it involved an immense amount of research, yet unlike some of his poems it is not overloaded with historical setting and local colour. In spite of the close knit argument there are frequent passages of poetic beauty and many sparkling phrases. One of the interspersed songs is specially notable. Not really relevant to the discussion either in the original or in this chapter, it is worth quoting as illustrating one of Browning's many facets and as an example of the verbal magic of which he was capable.

> Heap cassia, sandal-buds and stripes
>   Of labdanum, and aloe-balls,
> Smeared with dull nard an Indian wipes
>   From out her hair: such balsam falls
>   Down sea-side mountain pedestals,
> From tree-tops where tired winds are fain,
> Spent with the vast and howling main,
> To treasure half their island-gain.

---
[1] The influence of Shelley is clearly discernible both in the main theme and in some details. See, for example, *A Browning Handbook*, De Vane, pp. 47f.

THE ETERNAL PURPOSE

> And strew faint sweetness from some old
>   Egyptian's fine worm-eaten shroud
> Which breaks to dust when once unrolled;
>   Or shredded perfume, like a cloud
>   From closet long to quiet vowed,
> With mothed and dropping arras hung,
> Mouldering her lute and books among,
> As when a queen, long dead, was young.

Briefly put, the story tells how Paracelsus sets out, full of fierce energy and an arrogant self-sufficiency to acquire knowledge. All feeling must be cast behind him lest it interfere with his quest. Mind is his god and Learning the end of life. But experience disillusions him. In conversation with Aprile, a dying poet who has sought love and beauty as wholeheartedly as Paracelsus has sought knowledge, he comes to realize what each has missed. So the scholar cries to the poet:

> Love me henceforth, Aprile, while I learn
> To love; and, merciful God, forgive us both!
> We wake at length from weary dreams; but both
> Have slept in fairy-land: though dark and drear
> Appears the world before us, we no less
> Wake with our wrists and ankles jewelled still.
> I too have sought to KNOW as thou to LOVE—
> Excluding love as thou refusedst knowledge.
>
> . . . .
>
> Die not, Aprile! We must never part.
> Are we not halves of one dissevered world,
> Whom this strange chance unites once more? Part? never!
> Till thou the lover, know; and I, the knower,
> Love—until both are saved.

Aprile tries to say before he dies that what they seek can be found only in God, not through earthly love alone. But Paracelsus does not grasp this. He is still obsessed by pride and so love continues to elude him. In despair he gives up his ideals and plunges into a life of sensuality. The last scene shows him in delirium, with his friend Festus, the pastor, sitting beside his bed. He wakes to recognize him and pours out the tale of what he has learned from life. Not content with himself or his attainments he had at last sought joy in God. The wonderful description of God's joy in His self-giving in creation, quoted earlier,[1] comes in here and is followed by this:

> In my own heart love had not been made wise
> To trace love's faint beginnings in mankind,
> To know even hate is but a mask of love's,
> To see a good in evil, and a hope
> In ill-success; to sympathize, be proud
> Of their half-reasons, faint aspirings, dim
> Struggles for truth, their poorest fallacies,
> Their prejudice and fears and cares and doubts;
> All with a touch of nobleness, despite
> Their error, upward tending all though weak,
> Like plants in mines which never saw the sun,
> But dream of him, and guess where he may be,
> And do their best to climb and get to him.
> All this I knew not, and I failed.

Now he trusts that God in the new life he is entering will fulfil the aspirations of both Aprile and himself.

> If I stoop
> Into a dark tremendous sea of cloud
> It is but for a time; I press God's lamp
> Close to my breast, its splendour, soon or late
> Will pierce the gloom.

The whole poem is a kind of contest or dialogue between love and knowledge. Browning, as he often insists, believes with the Apostle Paul that knowledge in this life must be partial and will vanish away, but 'there are three things that last for ever: faith,

---

[1] See p. 49 above.

THE ETERNAL PURPOSE

hope and love; but the greatest of them all is love'.[1] This is how he puts it in A *Pillar at Sebzevar* in *Ferishtah's Fancies*, 1884,

> 'Friend,' quoth Ferishtah, 'all I seem to know
> Is—I know nothing save that love I can
> Boundlessly, endlessly. My curls were crowned
> In youth with knowledge,—off, alas, crown slipped
> Next moment, pushed by better knowledge still
> Which nowise proved more constant: gain, to-day,
> Was toppling loss to-morrow, lay at last
> —Knowledge, the golden?—lacquered ignorance!
> . . . .
> The prize is in the process: knowledge means
> Ever-renewed assurance by defeat
> That victory is somehow still to reach,
> But love is victory, the prize itself:

The question inevitably arises, what does Browning mean by 'love'? It is the most hard-worked and misused word in the language. Classical Greek has six words for 'love' in its different senses; in popular English usage the same word is made to cover an amazing range. It stands for the crudity of mere lust and the mush of the crooner and pop singer; the bitter-sweet ecstasies of the birth of love between man and woman, and the day-by-day loyalty of life-long comradeship 'for better for worse, for richer for poorer, in sickness and in health'. 'Love' can include the care of parent for child, the affection of friendship, the devotion of the patriot for his country, and the impulse that drives men to the succour of those in need. It can reach all the way from an egotistic exploitation of others for one's own pleasure to unselfish self-sacrifice. It can mean the love of God for man and man's answering love for Him. The Greek New Testament rejected altogether one of the classical words, *erōs*, because it had become tainted in pagan usage, and chose a rather colourless word.

[1] I Cor. 13.8, 9, 13 (NEB).

THE FAITH OF ROBERT BROWNING

agape, to fill it with Christian meaning. '*Agape* differs from *eros* in that the latter is brought into action by the attractiveness of the object loved, whereas *agape* loves even the unlovable, the repellent and those who have nothing to offer in return. It is thus a word which exactly describes God's attitude of free and utter grace.'[1]

In his wide-reaching studies of the ways of men and women Browning has described the emotions and behaviour of 'love' in all its senses, the degradations as well as the glories. But when he makes love the clue to the meaning of life and writes of the love of God for men, it is in Christ that he sees it demonstrated. And when he holds up the learning of love as the goal of human striving he is thinking of the reflection in the lives of men and women of that divine selfgiving. Love is essentially a relation between persons and does not exist as an abstraction.

7

It must be admitted that it is not easy to reconcile some of the poems in *Ferishtah's Fancies* published five years before his death, with the judgment advanced in this chapter as to his religious position. A series of fables told by an imaginary Persian dervish, who is, as he admitted, only a thin disguise for himself, this volume shows Browning still wrestling with problems of faith, perhaps too argumentatively to be good poetry. Taken by themselves these poems suggest a form of Theism. They cover a wide range, including providence, prayer, the use of human categories in speaking about God, asceticism, the ethics of punishment, and a defence of the necessity of permitting the presence of evil in the world. Dowden[2] not unfairly says the

---

[1] Alan Richardson, *Introduction to the Theology of the NT*, p. 269. There is a detailed analysis of the biblical meaning of Love in C. E. B. Cranfield's article in *The Theological Word Book of the Bible*.

[2] *Op. cit.*, p. 364.

book shows that Browning's 'early Christian faith has expanded and taken the non-historical form of a Humanitarian Theism, courageously accepted, not as a complete account of the Unknowable, but as the best provisional conception which we are competent to form. The theism involves rather than displaces the truth shadowed forth in the life of Christ'.

The Epilogue expresses a doubt whether his trust in God's goodness and love is not really only a reflection of the human love that had meant so much to him.

> Wide our world displays its worth, man's strife and strife's success :
> All the good and beauty, wonder crowning wonder,
> Till my heart and soul applaud perfection, nothing less.
> Only, at heart's utmost joy and triumph, terror
> Sudden turns the blood to ice : a chill wind disencharms
> All the late enchantment ! What if all be error—
> If the halo irised round my head were, Love, thine arms?

Elsewhere Browning has a vigorous answer to such arguments, holding that human love is itself irrefutable evidence of the reality of divine love. But here the question is left in the air. For all the vigour and humour of the poems they strike an uncertain note. The fables are by no means easy to interpret, and some of the interpretations students have seen in them do not fit at all with what he says elsewhere. There is a greater confidence and buoyancy in his next and last volume, *Asolando*, which might suggest his emergence from a passing period of perplexity.

8

In my judgment Browning cannot be claimed as a wholehearted adherent either by the orthodox evangelicals or by the unbelievers, who have both tried to enrol him on the strength of quotations torn from their context or taken out of relation to the total of his life and writings. He clearly had his moods of doubt and questioning, reflected most clearly in the words of the Pope who is generally thought to be expressing his own mature outlook. His faith was not lightly won or held. But there is no doubt where his compass needle pointed. Mrs Orr has a revealing remark: 'The evangelical Christian and the subjective idealist are curiously blended in his composition.'[1] This seems to me perceptive and penetrating and borne out by all the evidence. Sometimes these two elements proved uneasy neighbours, but in spite of all that has been urged to the contrary I am convinced Browning regarded himself as a Christian to the end of his days. At all times he was a deeply religious man. Perhaps not orthodox by some standards, at the very least he held to a Christian Theism. He believed love to be the fundamental truth about God, the guide and ground, so to say, of His power and wisdom. Jesus Christ, the historical figure, in His self-sacrifice for men was the messenger and expression of that love and the clue to the meaning of human life.

[1] *Op cit.*, p. 354.

IV

God in Christ

> I say the acknowledgment of God in Christ
> Accepted by thy reason, solves for thee
> All questions in the earth and out of it.
>
> *A Death in the Desert*

In a letter to William Temple's mother, George Wyndham says that Browning often read to him (Wyndham) and that 'he seemed to set the greatest store by *Karshish* and *A Death in the Desert*. If it is at all permissible to speak of so great an artist's "message"—a horrible phrase—his message is in those two poems. In another category he read with elation *Abt Vogler* and *The Last Ride Together*; in another with perfect dramatic intonation, *Bishop Blougram's Apology*; and lastly *A Toccata of Galuppi's* and *Up at a Villa* . . . He revelled in the speaker's view of the contrast between the villa and the city.'[1]

In this chapter we shall examine *Karshish* and *A Death in the Desert*, together with *Saul* and *Christmas Eve and Easter Day*, particularly from the point of view of Browning's beliefs about the Incarnation.

I

In the poem *Saul* the youthful David is trying to rouse Saul from his coma of apathy and distress. Through his playing and singing he seeks to reach the disordered mind. In his love he is willing to give all he has, but it is not enough. His spirit takes

---

[1] F. A. Iremonger, *Life of William Temple*, p. 48.

a leap towards God and he is compelled to a prophecy. All he has, including his love for Saul, is a gift from God and it is impossible that any gift should be greater than its Creator. God must have all David's love and more, and He has in addition the power to help that David lacks. God must surely express His love in some supreme act, through the Messiah, the Christ who is to come.

> Do I find love so full in my nature, God's ultimate gift,
> That I doubt his own love can compete with it? Here, the parts shift?
> Here, the creature surpass the Creator,—the end, what Began?
> Would I fain in my impotent yearning do all for this man,
> And dare doubt he alone shall not help him, who yet alone can?
>
> . . . .
>
> Would I suffer for him that I love? So wouldst thou—so wilt thou!
> So shall crown thee the topmost, ineffablest, uttermost crown—
> And thy love fill infinitude wholly
>
> . . . .
>
>   O Saul, it shall be
> A Face like my face that receives thee; a Man like to me,
> Thou shalt love and be loved by, for ever: a Hand like this hand
> Shall throw open the gates of new life to thee! See the Christ stand!

By the 'uttermost crown' of God, Browning meant, of course, the Incarnation and the self-giving of Jesus on Calvary, which the Pope, in an unforgettable phrase, calls a

>   transcendent act
> Besides which even the creation fades
> Into a puny exercise of power.[1]

[1] *The Ring and the Book.*

GOD IN CHRIST

2

A not dissimilar compulsion grips the sceptical mind of Karshish, the Arab physician. He is writing to his colleague, Abib, and has several matters of interest to communicate. He gives news of his further journeying from Jericho to Bethany and Jerusalem. He has found hints of new ways of treatment for two or three diseases and a better quality of gum-tragacanth. But he is obsessed by a strange case he met in Bethany of 'one Lazarus, a Jew'.

> The man had something in the look of him—
> His case has struck me far more than 'tis worth.
>
> 'Tis but a case of mania-subinduced
> By epilepsy, at the turning point
> Of trance prolonged unduly some three days.
>
> . . . The man's own firm conviction rests
> That he was dead (in fact they buried him)
> —That he was dead and then restored to life
> By a Nazarene physician of his tribe:
> —'Sayeth, the same bade 'Rise', and he did rise.

Lazarus is now in perfect bodily health, but shows strange symptoms of mental disorder. He has lost a proper sense of proportion. He carries on his daily work but pays no attention to things that are really important. For example, the whole country side is agog with the news that Vespasian is marching into Judea, but Lazarus does not care in the least.

> I probed the sore as thy disciple should:
> 'How, beast,' I said, 'this stolid carelessness
> 'Sufficeth thee, when Rome is on her march
> 'To stamp out like a little spark thy town,
> 'Thy tribe, thy crazy tale and thee at once?'
> He merely looked with his large eyes on me.

THE FAITH OF ROBERT BROWNING

> The man is apathetic, you deduce?
> Contrariwise, he loves both old and young,
> Able and weak, affects the very brutes
> And birds—how say I? flowers of the field—
> As a wise workman recognizes tools
> In a master's workshop, loving what they make.
> Thus is the man as harmless as a lamb:
> Only impatient, let him do his best,
> At ignorance and carelessness and sin—
> An indignation which is promptly curbed.

Karshish had, of course, tried to find the Nazarene healer to confer with him about the case, but he had 'perished in a tumult many years ago'.

> The other imputations must be lies;
> But take one though I loathe to give it thee.
>
> This man so cured regards the curer, then,
> As—God forgive me! who but God himself,
> Creator and sustainer of the world,
> That came and dwelt in flesh on it awhile!
> —'Sayeth that such an one was born and lived,
> Taught, healed the sick, broke bread at his own house,
> Then died, with Lazarus by, for aught I know,
> And yet was . . . what I said nor choose repeat,
> And must have so avouched himself, in fact,
> In hearing of this very Lazarus
> Who saith—but why all this of what he saith?
> Why write of trivial matters, things of price
> Calling at every moment for remark?
>
>   Thy pardon for this long and tedious case,
> Which, now that I review it, needs must seem
> Unduly dwelt on, prolixly set forth!
> Nor I myself discern in what is writ
> Good cause for the peculiar interest
> And awe indeed this man has touched me with.
> Jerusalem's repose shall make amends
> For time this letter wastes, thy time and mine;

GOD IN CHRIST

Till when, once more they pardon and farewell!

The very God! think, Abib, dost thou think?
So, the All-Great, were the All-Loving too—
So, through the thunder comes a human voice
Saying, 'O heart I made, a heart beats here!
Face, my hands fashioned, see it in myself!
Thou hast no power nor mayst conceive of mine,
But love I gave thee, with myself to love,
And thou must love Me who have died for thee!'
The madman saith He said so: it is strange.

3

In *Saul*, Old Testament faith looks forward in hope. In *Karshish* and *Cleon*[1] the Christian story is seen through pagan eyes. In *A Death in the Desert* Browning imagines how it looked to the apostle John at the end of a long life. William Temple said that this was his favourite of all Browning's poems and the best commentary on St John.[2] It imagines the aged apostle dying in a desert cave surrounded by rocky hills. He has been taken there by a small group of disciples to save him from the Roman persecution. He lies in the cool inner part of the cave, while 'outside was all noon and the burning blue'. Four men and a boy are with him. One, a Bactrian convert,

                    a wild, childish man
And could not write nor speak but only loved,
      . . . having his desire,
Kept watch, and made pretence to graze a goat
That gave us milk, on rags of various herb,
Plantain and quitch, the rocks' shade keeps alive:
So that if any thief or soldier passed,
(Because the persecution was aware)
Yielding the goat up promptly with his life,
Such man might pass on, joyful at a prize,
Nor care to pry into the cool o' the cave.

[1] See p. 96 below.
[2] Iremonger's *Life*, p. 176.

From time to time the Bactrian's cry is heard by the group telling them they are still safe.

At first John lies unconscious but eventually he rouses himself and tries to pass on to these converts the lessons of his life. These dying words are recorded by one of the group for the benefit of later generations. For the purposes of the poem we can accept Browning's apparent belief that the apostle wrote both the Fourth Gospel and the Book of Revelation, and the odd 'poetic licence' which credits him with foreknowledge of the 'philosophic doubt' of the nineteenth century as well as of the heresies of his own day.

John realizes that with his death will pass the last of those who saw and heard Jesus 'in the days of His flesh', and is concerned to know what he can say that will help coming generations who have not had that privilege. Experience of life and long pondering had made much luminous that had been dark, and he had come to understand the significance of much that had been puzzling.

> Since much that at the first, in deed and word,
> Lay simply and sufficiently exposed,
> Had grown (or else my soul was grown to match,
> Fed through such years, familiar with such light,
> Guarded and guided still to see and speak)
> Of new significance and fresh result;
> What first were guessed as points, I now knew stars,
> And named them in the Gospel I have writ.

It is all vividly present to him still.

> To me, that story—ay, that Life and Death
> Of which I wrote 'it was'—to me, it is;
> —Is, here and now: I apprehend nought else.
> Is not God now i' the world His power first made?
> Is not His love at issue still with sin
> Visibly when a wrong is done on earth?

GOD IN CHRIST

Nevertheless he is alive to the difficulties of the Christian Faith and to the attacks of the heretics. Spiritual truth is not like the facts of nature. Once man has learned the value of fire he will not part with it, but we do not grasp the value of Christ in the same way. Even he had to remember with shame how he had denied Christ.

> Sigh ye, 'It had been easier once than now'?
> To give you answer I am left alive;
> Look at me who was present from the first!
> Ye know what things I saw; then came a test,
> My first, befitting me who so had seen:
> 'Forsake the Christ thou sawest transfigured, Him
> 'Who trod the sea and brought the dead to life?'
> 'What should wring this from thee!'—ye laugh and ask.
> What wrung it? Even a torchlight and a noise.
> The sudden Roman faces, violent hands,
> And fear of what the Jews might do! Just that,
> And it is written, 'I forsook and fled:'

He imagines a critic of later days reading his Gospel, 'a tale of things done ages since', and wondering if such a person as John had ever existed at all, finding inaccuracies of detail, and wondering if after all it was not just a fable with a spiritual lesson. If miracles had ever happened, why did they not happen now? Had not universal law replaced belief in a personal God? And was not this story of love in God just a projection from our own experience of human love? The argument is intricate but perhaps John's answer may be summarized in these terms.

> I say that man was made to grow, not stop;
> That help, he needed once, and needs no more,
> Having grown but an inch by, is withdrawn:
>
> . . . .
>
> Man apprehends Him newly at each stage
> Whereat earth's ladder drops, its service done;
>
> . . . .

> I cried once, 'That ye may believe in Christ,
> 'Behold this blind man shall receive his sight!'
> I cry now, 'Urgest thou, *for I am shrewd*
> '*And smile at stories how John's word could cure—*
> '*Repeat that miracle and take my faith?*'
> I say, that miracle was duly wrought
> When, save for it, no faith was possible.

Miracles now, argues John, 'would compel not help': they have done their work. Man must learn and unlearn. He cannot expect ever to find complete certainty and it would not be good for him if he could.

> Such progress could no more attend his soul
> Were all it struggles after found at first
> And guesses changed to knowledge absolute.
> . . . .
> Man, therefore, thus conditioned, must expect
> He could not, what he knows now, know at first;
> What he considers that he knows to-day,
> Come but to-morrow, he will find misknown;
> Getting increase of knowledge, since he learns
> Because he lives, which is to be a man.

To say that our belief in the love of God is a mere projection from our own hearts and so to reject Christ, is like a lamp that is choked with too much oil, or a stomach that starves because it is stuffed too full with food. Man, 'appalled at nature', questions whether behind the power he saw in it there could be a loving person,

> He needed satisfaction God could give,
> And did give, as ye have the written word:
> . . . .
> But when, beholding that love everywhere,
> He reasons, 'Since such love is everywhere,
> 'And since ourselves can love and would be loved,
> 'We ourselves make the love, and Christ was not,'—

GOD IN CHRIST

> How shall ye help this man who knows himself,
> That he must love and would be loved again,
> Yet, owning his own love that proveth Christ,
> Rejecteth Christ through very need of Him?
> The lamp o'erswims with oil, the stomach flags
> Loaded with nurture, and that man's soul dies.
>
> . . . .
>
> I say, the acknowledgment of God in Christ
> Accepted by thy reason, solves for thee
> All questions in the earth and out of it,
>
> . . . .
>
> Then stand before that fact, that Life and Death,
> Stay there at gaze, till it dispart, dispread,
> As though a star should open out, all sides,
> Grow the world on you, as it is my world.

It is a moving poem and yields more the more one studies it, but I must confess that I do not find it altogether easy to grasp what the apostle, or Browning, is in the end saying to us, and the interpretations of commentators differ widely. In comparison, the next two poems we consider are straightforward.

4

Christmas Eve and Easter Day are two separate poems, though published at first in one volume. The first might be described as a commentary on the saying: 'Where two or three are gathered together in my name, there am I in the midst of them.' The second might be given the text: 'Without me ye can do nothing.' Fundamentally, perhaps, the narrator in both may be taken to represent Browning in the sense that they reveal his general outlook, though he cannot at all points be identified with the character he is describing.

Christmas Eve, in effect, surveys the main elements in the religious scene as he saw it in his day. Brought up a Dissenter, he never ceased to value the nonconformist heritage from seventeenth-century Geneva and the evangelical revival, though he was not at home in many of its expressions. He watched the influence of the Oxford Movement with suspicion, and in spite of his long residence in Italy, or perhaps because of it, he showed little understanding of, or sympathy for, Roman Catholicism. From the extreme critical movement of his day, threatening, as he believed, the very foundations of Christianity, he reacted violently. All this is reflected in *Christmas Eve* which takes us in turn to a dissenting chapel, St Peter's at Rome, and a lecture hall in Göttingen.

A storm drives the narrator to take shelter in a little dissenting mission hall. 'Mount Zion' is a caricature, drawn with the grim wit of which he was capable; it is not in the least typical of nonconformity in his day, or any other day, as he must have known well, though something like it might have been found in an undenominational mission hall in a poor district.[1] It was no doubt his intention to exaggerate, as he does when he comes to describe St Peter's. Building, congregation, and speaker are all unprepossessing. The atmosphere is foul and the congregation, drawn from 'a squalid knot of alleys' near by, is dirty and smelly. 'The preaching man's immense stupidity' is shown by the attempt 'with a patchwork of chapters and texts in severance' to prove the doctrine of the Trinity from Pharaoh's 'baker's dream of Baskets Three'. In utter disgust he flings out into the open air. Breathing it in and looking at the now clear sky, he reflects on the scene he had left.

> The sermon now—what a mingled weft
> Of good and ill!

There was a praiseworthy earnestness and a basis of truth, though deplorably presented. But how depressing the whole business was and how preferable the open air!

[1] He said himself that the description was completely 'imaginary'.

GOD IN CHRIST

> Oh, let men keep their ways
> Of seeking Thee in a narrow shrine.
> Be this my way!

Then on the path ahead of him he recognizes the figure of Christ! He too must just have left the mission hall. The saying that where two or three meet to pray He would be in the midst flashes into his mind. He is afraid Christ is going away from him because he had despised His friends, and he tries to justify himself:

> I thought it best that thou, the spirit,
> Be worshipped in spirit and in truth,
> And in beauty, as even we require it—
> Not in the forms burlesque, uncouth,
> I left but now, as scarcely fitted
> For thee . . .

In the middle of his excuses Christ gathers him into the folds of His garment and carries him off to St Peter's at Rome, 'that miraculous Dome of God'. Mass is being celebrated. He is impressed by the crowds, the music and the incense, but he cannot forget Rome's 'errors and perversities', though admitting that close inspection would show a spark of truth. He remains outside the door, as unsympathetic with the childish ritual and 'buffoonery' as with the dissenting sermon. The criticism is as crude and misunderstanding as the picture of the nonconformist chapel.[1]

But once again he is swept away, this time to a lecture room in Göttingen. The lecturer is even less to his taste than the crudities of Mount Zion or the 'posturings' of St Peter's.

> So, he proposed inquiring first
> Into the various sources whence
> This Myth of Christ is derivable;

[1] A more sympathetic attitude is shown in the portrait of the Pope in *The Ring and the Book*.

> Demanding from the evidence,
>   (Since plainly no such life was liveable)
> How these phenomena should class?
> Whether't were best opine Christ was,
> Or never was at all, or whether
> He was and was not, both together—
> It matters little for the name,
> So the idea be left the same.

His caricature of the professor dissolving Christ into a myth is surprisingly gentle, for Browning was clear that if the story of Jesus be proved a fable little of value would be left in Christianity. Even the destructive scholar partially recaptures his sympathy at the end of his lecture, though he is not sure how to greet the announcement. The professor advised his hearers to:

> 'Go home and venerate the myth
> 'I thus have experimented with—
> 'This man, continue to adore him
> 'Rather than all who went before him,
> And all who ever followed after!'—
> Surely for this I may praise you, my brother!
> Will you take the praise in tears or laughter?

What his vision, or dream, has nevertheless taught him is that where love is Christ is. Love with defective education or culture is worth more than knowledge lacking love. He feels rather proud of this 'genial mood' of tolerance.

> One trims the bark 'twixt shoal and shelf,
>   And sees, each side, the good effects of it,
> A value for religion's self,
>   A carelessness about the sects of it.
> Let me enjoy my own conviction,
>   Not watch my neighbour's faith with fretfulness,
> Still spying there some dereliction
>   Of truth, perversity, forgetfulness!
> Better a mild indifferentism.

But he recoils from this 'this lazy glow of benevolence'. There must be a best way of worship and we must endeavour to discover it. He prays that Pope and Professor may find Christ too,

> Meantime, I can but testify
> God's care for me—no more, can I.
> It is but for myself I know; . . .
> Meantime, in the still recurring fear
> Lest myself, at unawares, be found,
> While attacking the choice of my neighbours round
> With none of my own made—I choose here!

For suddenly he was back in the dismal chapel to find the sermon ending. Could he have been asleep? Certainly the way his neighbours are eying him suggests that.

He tries to sum up his impressions. The preacher undoubtedly was full of faults, yet he was at least offering genuine water to meet human thirst, though 'mingled with the taints of earth'. It was clearly helping the poor wrecks of humanity in the congregation.

> I then, in ignorance and weakness,
> Taking God's help, have attained to think
>   My heart does best to receive in meekness
> That mode of worship, as most of His mind,
> Where earthly aids being cast behind,
> His All in All appears serene
> With the thinnest human veil between,
> Letting the mystic lamps, the seven,
>   The many motions of his spirit,
> Pass, as they list, to earth from heaven.
>   For the preacher's merit or demerit,
> It were to be wished the flaws were fewer
>   In the earthen vessel, holding treasure
> Which lies as safe in a golden ewer;
>   But the main thing is, does it hold good measure?
> Heaven soon sets right all other matters!—
>   Ask, else, these ruins of humanity,

> This flesh worn out to rags and tatters,
>   This soul at struggle with insanity,
> Who thence take comfort—can I doubt?—
> Which an empire gained, were a loss without.
> May it be mine! And let us hope
> That no worse blessing befall the Pope.

If *Christmas Eve* was intended as a serious study of the three creeds of his generation the treatment is open to serious criticism as superficial and unjust to all three. Some critics have dismissed the whole poem with scorn both for form and content. It is certainly not one of his most impressive, even if we are in sympathy with his main contention. Nor does the metre chosen, with its clever and tricky rhyming, seem suitable for a serious subject, as Browning himself apparently felt, judging from his apology at the end.

> I have done: and if any blames me
> Thinking that merely to touch in brevity
>   The topics I dwell on, were unlawful,—
> Or worse, that I trench, with undue levity,
>   On the bounds of the holy and the awful,—
> I praise the heart, and pity the head of him,
> And refer myself to THEE, instead of him,
> Who head and heart alike discernest,
>   Looking below light speech we utter,
>   When frothy spume and frequent sputter
> Prove that the soul's depths boil in earnest!

In contrast, *Easter Day* is concerned with personal religion, God and the individual soul. The theme is stated at the outset:

> How very hard it is to be
> A Christian! Hard for you and me,
> —Not the mere task of making real
> That duty up to its ideal,
> Effecting thus, complete and whole,
> A purpose of the human soul—

> For that is always hard to do;
> But hard, I mean, for me and you
> To realize it, more or less,
> With even the moderate success
> Which commonly repays our strife
> To carry out the aims of life.

The poem discusses the difficulties of belief and of the practice of the Christian way of life, without any of the humour and lightness of touch found in *Christmas Eve*. In places the argument is not easy to follow. It may help a reader to realize that the words of the second speaker, the sceptic, are enclosed in quotation marks: those of the first speaker have none.

It is a conversation between a believer perplexed by the difficulties of living up to his Faith, and one whom we may for convenience call the sceptic, who has considerable doubts about the credibility of Christianity and of its relevance to the real conduct of human life. If only he could believe, says the sceptic, there would be little difficulty with the practice. Martyrdom would be a small price to pay for an eternity of joy, if only one could believe in it.

> 'Could I believe once thoroughly,
> 'The rest were simple. What? Am I
> 'An idiot, do you think,—a beast?
> 'Prove to me, only that the least
> 'Command of God is God's indeed,
> 'And what injunction shall I need
> 'To pay obedience? Death so nigh,
> 'When time must end, eternity
> 'Begin,—and cannot I compute,
> 'Weight loss and gain together, suit
> 'My actions to the balance drawn,
> 'And give my body to be sawn
> 'Asunder, hacked in pieces, tied
> 'To horses, stoned, burned, crucified,

> 'Like any martyr of the list?
> 'How gladly!—if I make acquist,
> 'Through the brief minute's fierce annoy,
> 'Of God's eternity of joy.
>
> '. . . So, I would rest content
> 'With a mere probability,
> 'But, probable; the chance must lie
> 'Clear on one side,—lie all in rough,
> 'So long as there be just enough
> 'To pin my faith to . . .'

There is evidence enough, retorts the believer, for those who really want it. The serious difficulty lies in following the command to 'renounce the world'. It is not so simple as you think and not a question of a quick martyrdom.

> But there be certain words, broad, plain,
> Uttered again and yet again,
> Hard to mistake or overgloss—
> Announcing this world's gain for loss,
> And bidding us reject the same:
> The whole world lieth (they proclaim)
> In wickedness,—come out of it!

Mrs Browning said the emphasis of the poem was ascetic—though she assured a correspondent that Robert had not taken to wearing a hair shirt! Browning himself replied that he was only stating one side of the case, which is a further proof that he did not identify himself with either of the speakers: he probably had some sympathy with both. The debate was in his own mind.

Well, retorts the sceptic, as for 'renouncing the world' there are those who give up everything most folk value in order to collect beetles or snuff-boxes.

> 'So that, subduing, as you want,
> 'Whatever stands predominant

GOD IN CHRIST

> 'Among my earthly appetites
> 'For tastes and smells and sounds and sights,
> 'I shall be doing that alone,
> 'To gain a palm-branch and a throne.
> 'Which fifty people undertake
> 'To do, and gladly, for the sake
> 'Of giving a Semitic guess,
> 'Or playing pawns at blindfold chess.'

But, replies the shaky believer, what if after all we are making a mistake and 'renounce life for the sake of death and nothing else?' The others could claim that they at least had their beetles and their snuff-boxes! We can only comfort ourselves by recognizing that faith in its very nature is a venture, like a grasshopper's leap—which once more shows how hard it is to be a Christian.

The sceptic, not unnaturally, does not find this very helpful. So the believer goes on to tell of a remarkable experience he had had three years before. Out walking, he was musing about the kind of issues they were discussing, and asked himself what kind of a showing he would make if he fell dead there and then and had to face his Judge.

> And as I said
> This nonsense, throwing back my head
> With light complacent laugh, I found
> Suddenly all the midnight round
> One fire.

It was in very fact Judgment Day, and he describes how he watched in fear and awe the fire sweeping over all things. Then a Voice spoke beside him:

> Life is done.
> Time ends. Eternity's begun.
> And thou art judged for evermore

Then 'He stood there' and the narrator fell at His feet. He was told that since throughout his life he had chosen the good things of earth and not of the spirit, he was condemned now to have them for ever and be shut out of the heaven of spirit.

The story-teller rejoiced in the verdict: no harsh sentence this. Everything around seemed as if no Judgment Day had been. He revelled in the thought of all the wealth of life open to him and set out to feast upon the joys of earth. In turn he explored the beauties and treasures of nature, art and intellect. But in turn they failed him. Divorced from the spirit he found them empty. So he cried to God that he would let the world go and choose love instead, so that life might once again have meaning. 'At last!' said the Judge. Love has always been there in the world if you had cared to look for it.

> 'Is this thy final choice?
> 'Love is the best? 'T is somewhat late!
> 'And all thou dost enumerate
> 'Of power and beauty in the world,
> 'The mightiness of love was curled
> 'Inextricably round about.
> 'Love lay within it and without,
> 'To clasp thee,—but in vain! Thy soul
> 'Still shrunk from Him who made the whole,
> 'Still set deliberate aside
> 'His love!—Now take love! Well betide
> 'Thy tardy conscience! Haste to take
> 'The show of love for the name's sake,
> 'Remembering every moment Who,
> 'Beside creating thee unto
> 'These ends, and these for thee, was said
> 'To undergo death in thy stead
> 'In flesh like thine: so ran the tale.
> 'What doubt in thee could countervail
> 'Belief in it? Upon the ground
> ' "That in the story had been found

GOD IN CHRIST

'"Too much love! How could God love so?"
'He who in all his works below
'Adapted to the needs of man,
'Made love the basis of the plan,—
'Did love, as was demonstrated:
'While man, who was so fit instead
'To hate, as every day gave proof,—
'Man thought man, for his kind's behoof,
'Both could and did invent that scheme
'Of perfect love.'

In deep shame the man begged to be allowed to go back to his old life with all its limitations and all its darkness, toil and sorrow, that he might struggle on and hope to attain a better. Then the Judge revealed Himself as Saviour, and removed the ban. The narrator recovered consciousness. Perhaps it had been all a dream, but at least life had become new.

And so I live, you see,
Go through the world, try, prove, reject,
Prefer, still struggling to effect
My warfare; happy that I can
Be crossed and thwarted as a man,
Not left in God's contempt apart,
With ghastly smooth life, dead at heart,
Tame in earth's paddock as her prize.

He still finds it hard to be a Christian, but he knows now that the grace of God is there to aid him.

But Easter-Day breaks! But
Christ rises! Mercy every way
Is infinite,—and who can say?

Fourteen years later Browning wrote the Epilogue to *Dramatis Personae*. There are three speakers. David describes Old Testament worship with its solemn and ordered Temple rites. Then

Renan speaks for nineteenth century scepticism and laments the passing of faith. The Face that once looked down on men has been 'lost in the night'. The third speaker is no doubt Robert Browning himself. He does not find help in ritualistic worship, nor does he stand with Renan.

> That one Face, far from vanish, rather grows,
> Or decomposes but to recompose,
> Become my universe that feels and knows.

When he read this to his friend, Mrs Orr, he said, 'The Face is the face of Christ. That is how I feel Him'.[1]

[1] Mrs Orr in *Contemporary Review*, Dec. 1891, p. 880.

V

The Mystery of Evil

This dread machinery of sin and sorrow.
The Ring and the Book

Was Browning an 'optimist'? The label has been applied to him by both friend and foe; by his admirers as one of his chief claims to praise and by his critics with a sneer. There is little doubt that his alleged optimism is one of the main reasons why people have turned from him since the first world war. How dare a man be optimistic in so grim and bitter-tasting a world as this! ' "God's in His heaven. All's right with the world." Indeed! What a thing to say! "Greet the unknown with a cheer." Well really! It is is clear that Browning lived before the days of the hydrogen bomb': so this generation thinks. It is perhaps not strange, though deplorable, that many moderns confuse pessimism and cynicism with wisdom, and dismiss 'optimism' as puerile superficiality and insensitivity.

Let two speak for many. F. L. Lucas writes of 'that complacent and obtuse satisfaction with human life which Browning once flaunted'.[1] Even as long ago as 1899 Dean Inge could write: 'It is easy to say with Browning, "God's in His heaven: all's right with the world" . . . but it would require a robust confidence or a hard heart to maintain this proposition while standing among the ruins of an Armenian village or by the deathbed of

---

[1] Quoted by Somervell, *op. cit.*

THE FAITH OF ROBERT BROWNING

innocence betrayed.'[1] Is Browning, then, guilty of 'complacent and obtuse satisfaction with human life'? Did he possess a hard heart? The charge must be examined.

Let us begin by clearing up this business about 'God's in His heaven'—apparently the only bit of Browning that many people know; and unfortunately they have got it all wrong.

> The year's at the spring
> And day's at the morn;
> Morning's at seven;
> The hill-side's dew-pearled;
> The lark's on the wing;
> The snail's on the thorn:
> God's in his heaven—
> All's right with the world!

This is not 'Browning' at all! It is the song of one of his imaginary characters, a little mill girl with all the innocence of youth, as she sets out for a day's holiday on a beautiful spring morning. She has nothing to do but enjoy herself for all the rest of the day and she is overflowing with happiness. Everything is lovely! And why not? It would be absurd to condemn Pippa for feeling like that. The song is entirely fitting on her lips: to condemn her creator for putting it there is doubly ludicrous.

Of course if that were the sum-total of Browning's considered judgment of life he would not be worth bothering about. If that was really all he had to say, he would deserve condemnation for a facile and unworthy attitude. But to produce this quotation as evidence of Browning's 'optimism', as is constantly done, is merely to be silly. In fact, it is only necessary to read the rest of this same poem to be confronted with all the cynic could desire—the cruellest of tricks played on a young man by the hatred of his companions, adultery, political assassination, murder and the

---

[1] *Christian Mysticism*, p. 54.

THE MYSTERY OF EVIL

plotting of murder. *Pippa Passes* has in fact a considerable bearing on Browning's beliefs about the meaning of pain and evil and may conveniently be looked at now.

The poem is a gripping story, finely presented, an artistic triumph ranging over both tragedy and comedy, the series of scenes being linked by the personality of the girl on holiday.

> To-morrow I must be Pippa who winds silk,
> The whole year round, to earn just bread and milk:
> But, this one day, I have leave to go,
> And play out my fancy's fullest games;
> I may fancy all day—and it shall be so—
> That I taste of the pleasures, am called by the names
> Of the Happiest Four in our Asolo!

Rising with the sun, eager not to miss a minute of the day, she wanders singing through the streets, imagining herself in the places of those whom she judges the most enviable people in the little town. As she passes their homes her songs float in at the windows with dramatic results, unknown to herself. Her 'happiest four' are in truth a very sordid or unromantic group and have all four arrived at moments of tragic importance.

Ottima, whose husband owns the mill where Pippa works, is with her lover, Sebald, who has killed her husband during the night. Rather like Lady Macbeth, she is trying to dispel his remorse when Pippa's light-hearted song strikes home to his conscience as the voice of judgment. He cries out

> 'God's in His heaven!' Do you hear that?
> Who spoke?

For him, this is no word of facile optimism. He sees himself naked in the sight of God. In self-loathing they both commit suicide.

When Pippa passes her next home, Jules and his bride have

just returned from their wedding and she pictures their happiness together. But Jules has discovered that he has been cruelly duped by his fellow students into marrying an ignorant girl of the lowest class instead of the refined and cultured woman of his dreams. He has determined to send her home at once with all the money he can scrape together, and to set off alone in his misery to start a new life elsewhere. When Pippa passes her song changes his resolve. After all, it is not the fault of his child-wife, Phene, who is distressed at what she has innocently done. He will keep her and educate her, and together they will grow into a glad comradeship.

Luigi, the third 'happy one', is with his mother. Pippa never knew her own father and mother and imagines how lovely it must be for them to be together. But Luigi is a patriot who believes he is called to serve his oppressed country by killing the Austrian emperor. Unknown to him, he has been betrayed and the Austrian police are on their way to surround the house. His mother is begging him to abandon his plan and he is on the verge of giving in to her when Pippa passes. Her song recalls him to his duty as he sees it, and he rushes from the house, so escaping the police.

The fourth of the imagined 'happy ones' is the bishop, who has come to Asolo to settle the affairs of his recently dead brother and is with the rascally servant who has stolen much of his brother's money. When threatened with exposure he reveals that Pippa is the child and heir of the brother, and proposes to the bishop that she should be sold to a brothel in Rome and the property divided between the bishop and himself. Just then Pippa passes, and the bishop recoils in horror and hands the scoundrel over to the police.

Pippa gets home at sunset. As she prepares for bed, quite unconscious of all she has done and escaped, she wonders if she will

THE MYSTERY OF EVIL

ever really come into contact with those with whom she has been identifying herself.

> Now, one thing I should like to really know:
> How near I ever might approach all these
> I only fancied being, this long day:
> —Approach, I mean, so as to touch them, so
> As to . . . in some way . . . move them—if you please,
> Do good or evil to them some slight way.
> For instance, if I wind
> Silk to-morrow, my silk may bind
> And border Ottima's cloak's hem.
> Ah me, and my important part with them,
> This morning's hymn half promised when I rose!
> True in some sense or other, I suppose.
> God bless me! I can pray no more to-night.
> No doubt, some way or other, hymns say right.
>
> *All service ranks the same with God—*
> *With God, whose puppets, best and worst,*
> *Are we: there is no last nor first.*

Much in the poem is beautiful and moving. Its power lies mostly in the contrast between the happy imaginings of the innocent child and the world of evil and intrigue which surrounds her. Browning sees her as an unconscious servant of God, illustrating one way in which He deals with evil.

It might indeed be argued that fundamentally Pippa is right. In the end of the day, while God remains in His heaven, all must be 'right with the world'. But if Browning held this as his ultimate belief, as a Christian must, it was not because he shut his eyes to the facts. No poet was ever more alive to the harsh realities. As Lascelles Abercrombie says: 'Browning could enter into and make himself the very mind and nerves and speech of evil while yet at the same time loathing it.'[1] His Guido, in *The Ring and the Book,* is a fit companion for Shakespeare's Iago for

[1] *Op cit.*, p. 86.

ruthless villainy. On a different level there are the horrible soliloquies of the two lawyers to whom the tragedy of Pompilia means just another professional job. In the sense intended by his critics Browning was never an 'optimist': rather an open-eyed realist. He found life here so mixed with evil and sorrow that he believed only a future life could make sense out of it.

What is an optimist? The *Concise Oxford Dictionary* says that optimism is (*a*) 'the doctrine that the actual world is the best of all possible worlds'. Browning believed that. Much of his argument, as we shall see, is directed to proving that God could not, so far as human judgment can see, have made the world otherwise if He meant it to be a training ground for men and women. He saw equally clearly that because of man's misuse of it the world as we know it is far from the best possible. (*b*) 'The view that good must ultimately prevail over evil in the universe.' Browning believed that too. It is one of the fundamental tenets of the Christian Faith. (*c*) 'A sanguine disposition, inclination to take bright views.' I am not sure if that was true of him. Certainly for most of his life he was a healthy man, abounding in energy, and inclined, some people thought, to be rather over-hearty. He enjoyed life. He would have no truck with the melancholy which Byron had made the poetic fashion. He makes his Shakespeare say, in *At the Mermaid*:

> Have you found your life distasteful?
>   My life did, and does, smack sweet.
> Was your youth of pleasure wasteful?
>   Mine I saved and hold complete.
> Do your joys with age diminish?
>   When mine fail me, I'll complain.
> Must in death your daylight finish?
>   My sun sets to rise again.
> I find earth not grey but rosy,
>   Heaven not grim but fair of hue.

THE MYSTERY OF EVIL

> Do I stoop? I pluck a posy.
> Do I stand and stare? All's blue.

But he had his days of depression, sorrow and doubt. One such seems to be behind the sad poem, *Fears and Scruples*, 1876, concerning the trials of faith in a world from which God is apparently absent. He certainly knew how hard life could be for others. Many of his critics have held that he was too fond of poring over the macabre, the unpleasant, the tragical: and his poetry is indeed full of them. In this at least he agreed with Thomas Hardy:

> If way to the Better there be, it exacts a full look at the worst.[1]

If Browning was an optimist in the true sense of the word, it was not merely a matter of temperament, or because he kept his eyes shut. It was due to a conviction about the ultimate nature of things, verified in his own experience, fortified by his heart and his mind, and finally based on the supreme fact of God in Christ. It was no morbid curiosity that made him study twisted natures, malice, cruelty, vice of every kind. Paracelsus speaks of a man he knew:

> No mean trick
> He left untried and well-nigh wormed
> All traces of God's finger out of him.

Browning pictures many such. He engages in an almost defiant parading of evil, while insisting on the triumph of good. One good reason for believing in Christianity is its realism.

---

[1] *In Tenebris*. Hardy, born 1840 and so twenty-eight years his junior, frequently met Browning and greatly admired his work, which had a considerable influence on his own poetry, though his fundamental outlook on life was very different. Hardy wrote to Edmund Gosse that he found Browning puzzling. How could a man of his quality cling to a faith 'worthy of a dissenting grocer'—why grocer, I wonder?

> The candid incline to surmise of late
>   That the Christian faith proves false, I find;
> For our Essays-and-Reviews' debate
>   Begins to tell on the public mind,
> And Colenso's words have weight:
>
> I still, to suppose it true, for my part,
>   See reasons and reasons; this, to begin:
> 'Tis the faith that launched point-blank her dart
>   At the head of a lie—taught Original Sin,
> The Corruption of Man's Heart.[1]

In several poems[2] he urges that without imperfection, failure, and at least the opportunity to sin, men might perhaps become angelic automatons, but they could not be men.

> Who speaks of man, then must not sever
> Man's very elements from man,
> Saying, 'But all is God's'—whose plan
> Was to create man and then leave him
> Able, his own word saith, to grieve him,
> But able to glorify him too,
> As a mere machine could never do,
> That prayed or praised, all unaware
> Of its fitness for aught but praise and prayer,
> Made perfect as a thing of course.[3]

Effort, failure, sorrow, even sin, are needed for the slow building of moral personality.

> 　　　　　　　　　　　In the eye of God
> Pain may have purpose and be justified.[4]

How could sympathy exist without pain? Evil is an inevitable counter to good, as darkness is to light.

---

[1] *Gold Hair*. The 'higher critical' views of Bishop Colenso and the writers of *Essays and Reviews* were widely regarded as destructive of Christian belief. See p. 48 above.
[2] Examples are *Abt Vogler, The Grammarian's Funeral, Rabbi ben Ezra, Andrea del Sarto, Prospice*.
[3] *Christmas Eve.*　　　　　　　　　　　[4] *Ferishtah's Fancies.*

THE MYSTERY OF EVIL

>   For me
> (Patience, beseech you!) knowledge can but be
> Of good by knowledge of good's opposite—
> Evil,—since, to distinguish wrong from right,
> Both must be known in each extreme, beside—
>   . . . Type need antitype
> As night needs day, as shine needs shade, so good
> Needs evil: how were pity understood
> Unless by pain?[1]

Browning was convinced that only through conflict could we come to know the good.

> Then, welcome each rebuff
> That turns earth's smoothness rough,
> Each sting that bids nor sit nor stand but go!
> Be our joys three-parts pain!
> Strive, and hold cheap the strain;
> Learn, nor account the pang; dare, never grudge the throe![2]

Only by fighting every inch of the way can man grow morally. As Bishop Blougram says:

> No, when the fight begins within himself,
> A man's worth something. God stoops o'er his head,
> Satan looks up between his feet—both tug—
> He's left, himself, i' the middle: the soul wakes
> And grows. Prolong that battle through his life!
> Never leave growing till the life to come!

So the Pope contemplating how the worldly priest, Caponsacchi, won his manhood through trial, exclaims:

>   Was the trial sore?
> Temptation sharp? Thank God a second time!
> Why comes temptation but for man to meet
> And master and make crouch beneath his foot,
> And so be pedestalled in triumph? Pray
> 'Lead us into no such temptations, Lord!'

[1] 'Francis Furini' in *Parleyings*.
[2] *Rabbi ben Ezra*.

> Yea, but, O Thou whose servants are the bold,
> Lead such temptations by the head and hair,
> Reluctant dragons, up to who dares fight,
> That so he may do battle and have praise!

Thus Browning held firmly that

> There is some soul of goodness in things evil,
> Would men observingly distil it out.[1]

But when put to the test men fail: they stumble and fall. To this he replies that failure does not really matter: we are judged by our aims and efforts, not by our achievements.

> For thence,—a paradox
> Which comforts while it mocks,—
> Shall life succeed in that it seems to fail:
> What I aspired to be,
> And was not, comforts me:
> A brute I might have been, but would not sink i' the scale.
>
> . . . .
>
> But all, the world's coarse thumb
> And finger failed to plumb
> So passed in making up the main account;
> All instincts immature,
> All purposes unsure,
> That weighed not as his work, yet swelled the man's amount:
>
> Thoughts hardly to be packed
> Into a narrow act,
> Fancies that broke through language and escaped;
> All I could never be,
> All, men ignored in me,
> This, I was worth to God, whose wheel the pitcher shaped.[2]

'What stops my despair?' asks David in *Saul* and answers:

> This;— 'tis not what man does which exalts him, but what man would do.

---

[1] Shakespeare, *Henry V*.
[2] *Rabbi ben Ezra*.

THE MYSTERY OF EVIL

Browning appears to go further and to believe in something like universal redemption. This could be illustrated from a number of poems. For example, after describing a visit to the Paris Morgue where he saw the pitiful remains of three drowned suicides, 'poor men God made, and all for that', he closes the poem, significantly called *Apparent Failure,* with the words:

> My own hope is, a sun will pierce
> The thickest cloud earth ever stretched;
> That, after Last, returns the First,
> Though a wide compass round be fetched;
> That what began best, can't end worst,
> Nor what God blessed once, prove accurst.

The sophistical Don Juan in *Fifine at the Fair* puts the point in a striking metaphor:

> Beneath the veriest ash, there hides a spark of soul
> Which, quickened by love's breath, may yet pervade the whole
> O' the grey, and, free again, be fire?—of worth the same,
> Howe'er produced, for, great or little, flame is flame.

There are hints that not even Ottima or Guido are beyond the reach of redemption.

Yet, though it is possible for a soul to see, 'by the means of Evil that Good is best',[1] we must never think that evil is good. Nothing rouses Browning's wrath so quickly as hesitancy or slackness, or sitting on the fence. We must choose: we must fight. 'Never again elude the choice of tints,' says the Pope to the reputed parents of Pompilia,

> White shall not neutralize the black, nor good
> Compensate bad in man, absolve him so:
> Life's business being just the terrible choice.

[1] *Old Pictures in Florence.*

THE FAITH OF ROBERT BROWNING

Sin is real: yet God is good and all-powerful. Man often chooses evil: and God permits it. Man sins and rebels against God: yet it is His will that all men should be saved. Here are dilemmas for all who think, and Browning was well aware of them. Only God can resolve the paradox. Reason cannot now fully substantiate the testimony of faith. Long pondering had convinced Browning that no completely satisfactory intellectual answer was possible. In a number of poems he reasons deeply about it all—and helpfully. But he is perhaps most convincing not as a logician but when he *sees* as a poet.

The pity and love which make men revolt against suffering and evil were implanted in them by their Creator, who must be at least as good as His creatures. The evil in the world is there to be overcome, and it can be overcome. Love is active in the world: and who put it there? One day love will have the irresistible power it deserves to have. That is the faith of Robert Browning. Into all this we shall probe yet more deeply as we proceed.

VI

After Death?

Truly there needs another life to come.

Paracelsus

I

In 1876 Browning wrote an impressive and revealing letter to a friend who believed herself to be dying and had written to thank him for the help of his poems.

> It is a great thing—the greatest—that a human being should have passed the probation of life and sum up its experience in a witness to the power and love of God. I dare congratulate you. All the help I can offer, in my poor degree, is the assurance that I see ever more reason to hold by the same hope, and that by no means in ignorance of what has been advanced to the contrary; and for your sake I would wish it to be true that I had so much of 'genius' as to permit the testimony of an especially privileged insight to come in aid of the ordinary argument. For I know I myself have been aware of the communication of something more subtle than a ratiocinative process when the convictions of 'genius' have thrilled my soul to its depths: as when Napoleon, shutting up the New Testament, said of Christ,—'Do you know that I am an understander of men? Well, He was no man.' Or as when Charles Lamb, in a gay fancy with some friends as to how he and they would feel if the greatest of the dead were to appear suddenly in flesh and blood once more, on the final suggestion, 'And if Christ entered this room?' changed his manner at once, and stuttered out, as his manner was when moved, 'You see, if Shakespeare entered we should all rise; if

THE FAITH OF ROBERT BROWNING

He appeared we must kneel'. Or, not to multiply instances, as when Dante wrote what I will transcribe from my wife's Testament, wherein I recorded it fourteen years ago,[1] 'Thus I believe, thus I affirm, thus I am certain it is, and that from this life I shall pass to another better, there, where that Lady lives of whom my soul was enamoured'.

Dear friend, I may have wearied you in spite of your goodwill. God bless you, sustain and receive you! Reciprocate this blessing with yours affectionately,

ROBERT BROWNING

He maintained throughout his life, though not without periods of questioning, that this life was unjust and irrational if there was no life to come. Yet science showed that the world of nature was rational, understandable by mind, so far as we could study it. Surely then it was only reasonable to argue that life must be reasonable throughout, that the discipline of human living must also have a purpose. But unless there was a future life much of the present one seemed futile. 'My foot is on the threshold of boundless life,' cries the dying Paracelsus.

> Truly there needs another life to come!
> If this be all—(I must tell Festus that)
> And other life await us not—for one,
> I say 't is a poor cheat, a stupid bungle,
> A wretched failure. I, for one, protest
> Against it, and I hurl it back with scorn.

He wrote that early in his life, at the age of twenty-three, and reiterated the same argument many times right through to its end.

2

In *Cleon* Browning described the pagan longing for assurance about the future. Cleon is depicted as a famous artist living on one of the Greek islands, a contemporary of the apostle Paul.

---

[1] I.e., when his wife died.

AFTER DEATH?

The poem is a reply to a letter from the king, Protus. Cleon praises him for his love of the arts and admits that, as the king says, he has himself been poet, sculptor, musician, painter and philosopher too. The king has written that Cleon must be accounted to have attained 'the very crown and proper end of life', and must be proud to know that he is leaving so much of himself behind in his works. The king, by contrast, says he is sadly conscious that he is leaving to posterity nothing memorable or enduring. Cleon replies that he is chiefly conscious of increasing age and growing inability to do or to enjoy, though he has unmet longings, and sees

>   a world of capability
> For joy, spread round us, meant for us,
> Inviting us . . .
>   Every day my sense of joy
> Grows more acute, my soul (intensified
> By power and insight) more enlarged, more keen;
> While every day my hairs fall more and more,
> My hand shakes, and the heavy years increase—
> The horror quickening still from year to year,
> The consummation coming past escape
> When I shall know most, and yet least enjoy—
> When all my works wherein I prove my worth,
> Being present still to mock me in men's mouths,
> Alive still, in the praise of such as thou,
> I, I the feeling, thinking, acting man,
> The man who loved his life so over much,
> Sleep in my urn. It is so horrible,
> I dare at times imagine to my need
> Some future state revealed to us by Zeus,
> Unlimited in capability
> For joy, as this is in desire for joy,
> —To seek which, . . .
> Freed by the throbbing impulse we call death,
> We burst there as the worm into the fly,
> Who, while a worm still, wants his wings. But no!

> Zeus has not yet revealed it; and alas,
> He must have done so, were it possible!

He is sorry he cannot tell the king where he can send a message to 'one called Paulus'. He had heard of him and indeed some disciples of his had landed at his island and

> preached him and Christ,
> And (as I gathered from a bystander)
> The doctrine could be held by no sane man.
> . . . .
> Thou wrongest our philosophy, O King,
> In stooping to inquire of such an one . . .

It is obviously inconceivable that Paul could have access to any secret knowledge not available to the culture of Greece.

In *Rabbi ben Ezra*, in sharp contrast, Browning presents the portrait of a triumphant old age. The rabbi sees it as a vantage point from which to survey his past, a time to gather the fruits of life. He has come to see that success or failure in life must be judged by spiritual standards, in terms of aspiration and effort, no less than by achievement.[1] He looks forward calmly to the summons of death.

> Grow old along with me!
> The best is yet to be,
> The last of life, for which the first was made:
> Our times are in His hand
> Who saith 'A whole I planned,
> Youth shows but half; trust God: see all nor be afraid!'
>
> Therefore I summon age
> To grant youth's heritage,
> Life's struggle having so far reached its term:
> Thence shall I pass, approved
> A man, for aye removed
> From the developed brute; a god though in the germ.

[1] See p. 92 above.

AFTER DEATH?

>And I shall thereupon
>Take rest, ere I be gone
>Once more on my adventure brave and new:
>Fearless and unperplexed,
>When I wage battle next,
>What weapons to select, what armour to indue.
>
>. . . . .
>
>So, take and use Thy work:
>Amend what flaws may lurk,
>What strain o' the stuff, what warpings past the aim!
>My times be in Thy hand!
>Perfect the cup as planned!
>Let age approve of youth, and death complete the same!

A *Grammarian's Funeral* develops the theme propounded by the Pope in *The Ring and the Book*,

>Life is probation and the earth no goal
>But starting point of man.

Failure or not, our work in this life will not be wasted. It will come into its own in the next world.

>Yea, this in him was the peculiar grace
>   (Hearten our chorus!)
>That before living he'd learn how to live—
>   No end to learning:
>Earn the means first—God surely will contrive
>   Use for our earning.
>Others mistrust and say, 'But time escapes:
>   'Live now or never!'
>He said, 'What's time? Leave Now for dogs and apes!
>   'Man has Forever.'

3

Browning's knowledge and love of music comes out in many of his poems. One of these bears directly on our present subject.

Abt Vogler,[1] a musician extemporizing on his organ, gives through his music substance to his hopes and certainty to the realities he could not see (to adapt the NEB version of Heb. 11.1). Like the angels and demons that Solomon summoned to his aid in the legend, the sounds he evokes lay the foundations and raise the walls of a soaring edifice—or, to change the metaphor, give him wings on which his soul mounts to heaven. Round him gather the spirits of 'the wonderful Dead who have passed through the body and gone', to whisper their messages to him. In a moment of vision the sounds combine to create more than just another sound—a God-given star.

> And I know not if, save in this, such gift he allowed to man
>   That out of three sounds he frame, not a fourth sound, but a star.

When the moment passes all his palace of music disappears with its 'cloud capped towers'. But the memory of it remains even when he drops again into the sober key of C major, back to everyday routine and drudgeries. Can anything so good be as ephemeral as his music? Surely not!

> There shall never be one lost good! What was, shall live as before;
>   The evil is null, is nought, is silence implying sound;
> What was good shall be good, with, for evil, so much good more;
>   On the earth the broken arcs; in the heaven, a perfect round.
> All we have willed or hoped or dreamed of good shall exist;
>   Not its semblance, but itself; no beauty, nor good, nor power
> Whose voice has gone forth, but each survives for the melodist
>   When eternity affirms the conception of an hour.
> The high that proved too high, the heroic for earth too hard,
>   The passion that left the ground to lose itself in the sky,

---

[1] 1749-1814. Court chaplain at Mannheim. Improved the structure of the organ. Visited London in 1790.

AFTER DEATH?

> Are music sent up to God by the lover and the bard;
>   Enough that he heard it once: we shall hear it by-and-by.

Music is a path to reality, a medium through which God speaks.

> Sorrow is hard to bear, and doubt is slow to clear,
> Each sufferer says his say, his scheme of the weal and woe;
> But God has a few of us whom He whispers in the ear;
> The rest may reason and welcome: 'tis we musicians know.

4

His fullest discussion of immortality, however, is contained in *La Saisiaz*, the name (meaning 'the sun') of a villa near Geneva where he spent a holiday in the summer of 1877. He was with his sister and a close friend of twenty-five years standing, Miss Egerton Smith. While preparing to join them for a mountain climb Miss Smith suddenly died of heart failure. The event was a great shock. In the following year, at the age of sixty-five, he published this long poem as the outcome of his wrestling with the mystery of death and the reality of a future life. Written in his own person it is not so much a logical argument as the record of the impact of a deeply moving experience.

It tells how, a lonely climber, he set out to make by himself the ascent they had intended to make with their friend. As he climbs he reflects on her departure and on what it means to die. He is determined to be honest with himself as to what he really believes.

> I will ask and have an answer,—with no favour, with no fear,—
> From myself. How much, how little, do I inwardly believe
> True that controverted doctrine? Is it fact to which I cleave,
> Is it fancy I but cherish, when I take upon my lips
> Phrase the solemn Tuscan[1] fashioned, and declare the soul's eclipse

[1] Dante, whose words are quoted above in Browning's letter to his friend.

Not the soul's extinction? take his 'I believe and I declare—
Certain am I—from this life I pass into a better, there
Where that lady lives of whom enamoured was my soul'—
　where this
Other lady, my companion dear and true, she also is?

He accepts the reality of God and the soul as the two inevitable postulates of human thought: they are beyond the need and possibility of proof. What follows? Is survival after death a necessary deduction? He is sure that this life, if it be everything, is irrational and an indictment of the wisdom and love of God. Life is grossly unfair. How often we see

Stalwart body idly yoked to stunted spirit, powers, that fain
Else would soar, condemned to grovel, groundlings through
　the fleshly chain.

To himself, on balance, life has brought more pain and sorrow than happiness.

I must say—or choke in silence—'Howsoever came my fate,
Sorrow did and joy did nowise,—life well weighed,—preponderate.'
By necessity ordained thus? I shall bear as best I can;
By a cause all-good, all-wise, all-potent? No, as I am man!
Such were God: and was it goodness that the good within my
　range
Or had evil in admixture or grew evil's self by change?
I have lived then, done and suffered, loved and hated, learnt
　and taught
This—there is no reconciling wisdom with a world distraught,
Goodness with triumphant evil, power with failure in the
　aim . . .
If you bar me from assuming earth to be a pupil's place,
And life, time—with all their chances changes,—just probation space.

Granted this, life becomes tolerable and intelligible.

AFTER DEATH?

> . . . Only grant a second life, I acquiesce
> In this present life as failure, count misfortune's worst assaults
> Triumph, not defeat, assured that loss so much the more exalts
> Gain about to be.

Good is known through evil, truth by being confronted by falsehood: the discipline is defensible if it is preparing for the future. Complete assurance of a future life would defeat the usefulness of this present one as a probation. But we do not need certainty.

> Hope the arrowy, just as constant, comes to pierce its gloom, compelled.
> By a power and by a purpose which, if no one else beheld
> I behold in life, so—hope!

Mrs Orr says that *La Saisiaz* conclusively proves that Browning was no Christian, because he says nothing here of the revelation in Christ. But he does elsewhere, as this book abundantly shows. It would be truer to say that he is here trying to see what can be argued for a belief in immortality on general grounds, as many Christian philosophers have done. Taken by itself, *La Saisiaz* offers no evidence one way or the other as to Browning's attitude to Christianity: for that we must look elsewhere.

He was probably influenced in his treatment of the subject by a series of articles by different writers on 'The Soul and the Future Life' which was appearing that very summer in *The Nineteenth Century*, and which Miss Smith and he had both been reading. He refers to this series in the poem. This is his contribution to the debate, which deliberately left on one side any argument from the Christian revelation.

5

In *Dramatis Personae*, published earlier in 1864, he had seen death as the last adversary and braced himself to meet it. Beyond it would come reunion with his beloved Elizabeth who had died just three years before. *Prospice* (i.e. 'Look ahead!') is one of his best known poems, but it can hardly be omitted here.

> Fear death?—to feel the fog in my throat,
>   The mist in my face,
> When the snows begin, and the blasts denote
>   I am nearing the place,
> The power of the night, the press of the storm,
>   The post of the foe;
> Where he stands, the Arch Fear in a visible form,
>   Yet the strong man must go:
> For the journey is done and the summit attained,
>   And the barriers fall,
> Though a battle's to fight ere the guerdon be gained,
>   The reward of it all.
> I was ever a fighter, so—one fight more,
>   The best and the last!
> I would hate that death bandaged my eyes, and forbore,
>   And bade me creep past.
> No! let me taste the whole of it, fare like my peers
>   The heroes of old,
> Bear the brunt, in a minute pay glad life's arrears
>   Of pain, darkness and cold.
> For sudden the worst turns the best to the brave,
>   The black minute's at end,
> And the elements' rage, the fiend-voices that rave,
>   Shall dwindle, shall blend,
> Shall change, shall become first a peace out of pain,
>   Then a light, then thy breast,
> O thou soul of my soul! I shall clasp thee again,
>   And with God be the rest!

In his last book of all, *Asolando*, in its last two poems, is the reaffirmation of his life-long faith, not always held without difficulty, but triumphant at the end. To the longer *Reverie*, in which he muses over the cumulative experience of life, we shall

AFTER DEATH?

return later. The *Epilogue*, his last published word, shows confidence as he faces the unseen, being then as ever, one who

> Never doubted clouds would break,
> Never dreamed, though right were worsted, wrong would triumph,
> Held we fall to rise, are baffled to fight better,
> Sleep to wake.

VII

The Ring and the Book[1]

~~~

Touched aright, prompt yields each particle its tongue
Of elemental flame—no matter whence flame sprung,
From gums and spice, or else from straws and rottenness.
Fifine at the Fair

On its first publication *The Athenaeum* wrote: 'We must record at once our conviction, not merely that *The Ring and the Book* is beyond all parallel the supremest poetical achievement of our time, but that it is the most precious and profound spiritual treasure that England has produced since the days of Shakespeare.' Many other journals were loud in its praise. The days of Browning's undeserved neglect were triumphantly over. Beyond all question it is his own greatest poem and one of the greatest in all English literature. In an enquiry such as we are making into his ethical and religious beliefs it is of the first importance. There have been references to it already in every chapter, but it also demands one to itself.

I

One day in June, 1860, Browning picked out a little square, yellow book from among the miscellaneous rubbish on a secondhand stall in Florence. It cost him eightpence, and contained printed and manuscript information about a once notorious trial

[1] I have made use in this chapter of material from an earlier book of mine, *Great Christian Books*, long out of print.

THE RING AND THE BOOK

arising out of a sordid case of murder. The book described itself, in Latin which he thus translates, as giving:

> Position of the entire criminal cause
> Of Guido Franceschini, nobleman,
> With certain Four the cutthroats in his pay,
> Tried, all five, and found guilty and put to death
> By heading or hanging as befitted ranks,
> At Rome on February Twenty Two,
> Since our salvation Sixteen Ninety Eight:
> Wherein it is disputed if, and when,
> Husbands may kill adulterous wives, yet 'scape
> The customary forfeit.

Later on in London, by some queer chance, he discovered another contemporary pamphlet giving additional facts. The story fascinated him. As Italian jewellers in making a ring mixed alloy with the gold, so he mingled his own imaginings with the facts and in 1868 produced *The Ring and the Book*. 'I fused my live soul and that inert stuff.'

Here, in brief, is the story itself. A middle-class couple in Rome, Pietro and Violante Comparini, managed to marry their young adopted daughter to a noble of fifty, Count Guido Franceschini. Their motive is to obtain an aristocratic alliance and to enter the fashionable world. The Count, on his part, expects a large dowry, to mend his fallen fortunes. Neither side consults the feelings of the child-wife Pompilia, who is sacrificed to the selfish greed of both parties. Pending the sale of their supposed properties in order to pay the dowry, the parents go to stay with their son-in-law at Arezzo. Disappointed at the dull country life, and their treatment in a household where it is scarcely possible to make ends meet, they indignantly return to Rome. The youthful Pompilia has nothing in common with her mean and cruel husband, who vents upon her his rage at discovering that she is not the daughter of her reputed parents and that no money is likely to be forthcoming. After suffering all kinds of humiliating experiences, Pompilia determines to join her friends in Rome and is aided in escaping by a young priest, Canon Caponsacchi. Guido pursues and overtakes them, has them arrested, and institutes divorce proceedings. He is met by a counter-suit on the ground of his cruelty. The Court leans to the wife's side. Her flight was judged hasty and compromising, though the charge of infidelity is held unproved. Merely nominal punishment is meted out. Pompilia is sent to a convent for a time and Caponsacchi is temporarily banished to a distant town.

Guido retires to Arezzo, discomfited and angry, to meet the jeers and contempt of his acquaintances. A few months later he hears that his wife has given birth to a son. Moved by ungovernable rage, he determines to wipe out what he pretends to regard as a blot on his good name. He hires assassins, proceeds to Rome, kills Pietro and Violante and fatally wounds Pompilia, though she lives long enough to give her version of the story and to prove the guilt of her husband. His plea that he was avenging the wrong done to him by his wife's adultery with the priest is shown to be false, and it is revealed that he himself had plotted to throw them together in order to win his freedom. He appeals from his judges to the Pope, who reviews the whole case but confirms the sentence of death.

The poem consists of twelve books in which this story is told and retold from the standpoints of the chief actors and the onlookers. Half-Rome sides with Guido: the Other Half-Rome takes Pompilia's part. Tertium Quid, a superior person, supercilious and cynical, goes over the affair with a fashionable group. So far it has been a versified tale, with but little poetry. But then the story takes added force and fire as the Count, Capon-

THE RING AND THE BOOK

sacchi and Pompilia give their versions. The leading lawyers on either side rehearse their pleas in detached, professional spirit. The Pope's searching, sympathetic and profound analysis follows. Then the Count, sentenced and desperate, once more pleads his cause, and an epilogue rounds off the whole.

Soon after publication Carlyle hailed the author with enthusiastic praise, not unmingled with irony: 'What a wonderful fellow you are, Browning! You have written a whole series of books about what could be summed up in a newspaper paragraph.' That was just Carlyle's little joke, but even the Browning enthusiast may wish the poem shorter. Browning was apt to be long-winded, and for all its genius, *The Ring and the Book* would gain by pruning. Witty as they are, the descriptions of the lawyers' speeches are wearisomely long, and both these books might be passed over without losing anything essential to the argument. Yet it is an amazing feat to tell the same story ten times over from the standpoint of different persons, preserving the individuality of each in vivid and life-like fashion. To each monologue the poet's art brings a fitting variety of style suited to the speaker, a cunning adaptation of language and even of rhythm, a choice of figures of speech matching the experience and calibre of mind of each. This method of dramatic monologue is, as we have seen, one which Browning had made peculiarly his own.

The tragedy is thus 'reconstructed', as the writers of detective stories say—and this is a kind of detective story—by the actors in it and by those who observe from the outskirts. The characters grow as we watch them. Pompilia develops from a child into a woman, as her cruel experience brings out the slumbering qualities of her nature, her innate modesty and sweetness of disposition. Guido changes from a loutish country squire into a man of action under the stress of his wrongs, real and feigned, and the frustration of his selfish plots; becoming soured, cross-grained, implacably cruel. While Caponsacchi has the latent chivalry of his nature roused by the simple purity of the woman who begs his help; the frivolous priestling achieves a strong manhood. Let us follow the story rather more closely as Browning unfolds it.

After the introductory outline he shows us one Half-Rome siding with the husband. The Count, they hold, is more sinned against than sinning. A proud, sensitive man of noble family but fallen fortunes, he had danced attendance for many years on those who might have given him opportunity for advancement. Tired and hopeless, he determined to retire to Arezzo to end his days in peace and simplicity of life. But his brother Paul counsels him to marry a wife with money and offers to find him a suitable match. Designing parents trap him into marriage by promises of a rich dowry, but the dowry does not materialize and he finds himself maintaining the parents as well as the daughter. Disgusted with the frugal fare and the dull life the parents return to Rome, full of tales of his meanness. Once there they declare that Pompilia is not their daughter at all, but the child of a prostitute whom they had adopted, and that therefore any promise of a dowry is null and void. The Count tries to make the best of it, but his young wife carries on intrigues, especially with a handsome priest with whom she eventually runs away. Guido pursues and has them arrested. But the Court lets them off with a mere show of punishment, holding the charge of adultery unproven. The wretched Count is further goaded by a counter-charge for divorce on the grounds of his cruelty and then by the birth of a child falsely alleged to be his. Naturally he takes the law into his own hands and in a fit of rage kills father, mother and daughter. If he is to be condemned for this, there is no justice in Rome.

THE RING AND THE BOOK

The Other Half-Rome sides with Pompilia, who has been throughout the victim of other people's wickedness. The mother was certainly guilty of sharp practice, but she acted from the best of motives. The Count cared for nothing but the dowry, and treated the parents abominably. Little wonder they returned to Rome and tried to get their own back. Guido had then poured out his wrath on his luckless child-wife, who at least was innocent of any crime. He had plotted to drive her into misconduct to justify divorce. At last she flees with the help of a friend whom she has scarcely seen, but who has been described to her as a kindly, resolute man who would take pity on her misfortune. The charge of infidelity is a trumped up lie. Guido is a low scoundrel and the world will be well rid of him.

Tertium Quid, a third party, sits on the fence; it is hard to tell where the truth lies. Flippant and aristocratic, he surveys the tragedy with detachment and is sure a good deal of the trouble was caused by the Count getting mixed up with such plebeian folk at all.

Next come the three chief parties in the case. Guido and Caponsacchi are addressing the judges, the former after having been put to question on the rack. Pompilia is talking to a group round her bed in the convent, where wounded and dying, she is being cared for.

Under torture Guido has confessed the murders and is seeking to set the undeniable fact in the best light he can. No romantic villain this:

> A beak-nosed, bushy-bearded, black-haired lord,
> Lean, pallid, low of stature yet robust,
> Fifty years old.

Twisting every incident to suit his case, and standing upon his rights as a husband and the head of a noble house, he slurs over this and emphasizes that, adapting himself to his audience of ecclesiastics in the most artful and plausible fashion. He talks piously and with much appeal to sentiment, and presents his deed as a vindication of his honour and a defence of the sacred institution of marriage itself.

A very different story is Caponsacchi's, instinct with suppressed indignation and at times with uncontrollable eloquence. From the moment when he first set eyes on Pompilia in the theatre,

> A lady, young, tall, beautiful, strange and sad,

he was solemnized and awed, with a kind of worship that quickened his frivolous nature to self-sacrifice. He passionately defends Pompilia and himself from any vestige of unworthy motive. He had spoken to her only once, when she had appealed to him for help in such a way that he could not refuse to respond. Throughout he had been moved only by compassion. Guido, by the intermediary of a maid, had tried to entrap him into an intrigue with Pompilia, a trick which he had indignantly rejected. In flaming language he shrivels up the calumnies.

In striking contrast to this fiery eloquence come the opening words from Pompilia's death-bed:

> I am just seventeen years and five months old,
> And, if I lived one day more, three full weeks;
> 'T is writ so in the church's register,
> Lorenzo in Lucina, all my names
> At length, so many names for one poor child,
> —Francesca Camilla Vittoria Angela
> Pompilia Comparini,—laughable!
> Also 't is writ that I was married there
> Four years ago: and they will add, I hope,
> When they insert my death, a word or two,—
> Omitting all about the mode of death,—
> This, in its place, this which one cares to know,

THE RING AND THE BOOK

> That I had been a mother of a son
> Exactly two weeks

As she lies dying her life with all its pleasures and pains 'looks old, fantastic and impossible'. Two gifts remain to her, her baby and the friend who had rescued her.

> Oh how good God is that my babe was born,
> —Better than born, baptized and hid away
> Before this happened, safe from being hurt!
> That had been sin God could not well forgive:
> He was too young to smile and save himself . . .
> A whole long fortnight: in a life like mine
> A fortnight filled with bliss is long and much.
> All women are not mothers of a boy,
> Though they live twice the length of my whole life,
> And, as they fancy, happily all the same.
> There I lay, then, all my great fortnight long,
> As if it would continue, broaden out
> Happily more and more, and lead to heaven:
> Christmas before me,—was not that a chance?
> I never realized God's birth before—
> How He grew likest God in being born.
> This time I felt like Mary, had my babe
> Lying a little on my breast like hers.

She declares her forgiveness for 'that most woeful man, my husband once'.

> We shall not meet in this world nor the next,
> But where will God be absent? In His face
> Is light, but in His shadow healing too:
> Let Guido touch the shadow and be healed!

Peace has come at the close of her sad life.

> One cannot judge
> Of what has been the ill or well of life,
> The day that one is dying,—sorrows change
> Into not altogether sorrow-like;

> I do see strangeness but scarce misery,
> Now it is over, and no danger more.
> . . . .
> Yes, everybody that leaves life sees all
> Softened and bettered . . .
> To me at least was never evening yet
> But seemed far beautifuller than its day,
> For past is past.

Her last words are of gratitude to Caponsacchi, 'my one friend, my only, all my own, who put his breast between the spears and me'.

> O lover of my life, O soldier-saint,
> No work begun shall ever pause for death!
> Love will be helpful to me more and more
> I' the coming course, the new path I must tread—
> My weak hand in thy strong hand, strong for that! . . .
> My fate
> Will have been hard for even him to bear:
> Let it confirm him in the trust of God,
> Showing how holily he dared the deed!
> . . . .
> He is a priest;
> He cannot marry therefore, which is right:
> I think he would not marry if he could.
> Marriage on earth seems such a counterfeit,
> Mere imitation of the inimitable:
> In heaven we have the real and true and sure . . .
> So, let him wait God's instant men call years;
> Meantime hold hard by truth and his great soul,
> Do out the duty! Through such souls alone
> God stooping shows sufficient of His light
> For us i' the dark to rise by. And I rise.

The whole picture of Pompilia is unforgettable, a tale, in Swinburne's words, of 'piercing and overpowering tenderness'.

For present purposes we can pass over the rival lawyers, and turn to the Pope's final verdict, for Guido has appealed to him, pleading 'benefit of clergy' on the strength of some minor ecclesiastical office. It is generally agreed that we may see in the Pope's soliloquy not only Browning's own view of the tragedy, but an exposition, though couched in terms proper to the Pope, of much of the author's own Christian philosophy of life. Poetically the finest of all the books, it presents the judgment of a man wise by long experience in all the secrets of the human soul. Innocent the Twelfth,

> Simple, sagacious, mild yet resolute,
> With prudence, probity and—what beside
> From the other world he feels impress at times,
> Having attained to fourscore years and six—

has been studying the case from early morning, and now in

>   the dim
> Droop of a sombre February day
> In the plain closet where he does such work,
> With, from all Peter's treasury, one stool,
> One table and one lathen crucifix,

he sums up his findings. Pompilia he pronounces faultless, a rose all the more beautiful because of the dung heap from which it sprang. Caponsacchi is not without blame, but yet a true soldier of Christ courageously daring a difficult task, and nobly resisting the temptations put in his way. Guido has been doubly wicked, not only in the brutal murder, but in imperilling his wife's soul by placing temptation in her path. For him he can see no excuse and little hope of penitence and salvation. The prospect is all black, but perhaps even here the light of God may penetrate.

> For the main criminal I have no hope
> Except in such a suddenness of fate.

> I stood at Naples once, a night so dark
> I could have scarce conjectured there was earth
> Anywhere, sky or sea or world at all:
> But the night's black was burst through by a blaze—
> Thunder struck blow on blow, earth groaned and bore,
> Through her whole length of mountain visible:
> There lay the city thick and plain with spires,
> And, like a ghost disshrouded, white the sea.
> So may the truth be flashed out by one blow,
> And Guido see, one instant, and be saved.
> Else I avert my face, nor follow him
> Into that sad obscure sequestered state
> Where God unmakes but to remake the soul
> He else made first in vain; which must not be.
> Enough, for I may die this very night
> And how should I dare die, this man let live?

Reluctantly, yet confident that he is doing his duty, he signs the warrant for the execution.

Then once more we see Guido, now in the condemned cell. A cardinal and a priest are there to tell him of the sentence and hear his last confession before he goes to the scaffold. Guido throws off the mask. He is no longer the suave, cringing devotee of the Church, pleading for his life. Now he pours out a wild flood of entreaty, defiance and blasphemy. The last desperate scream as the officers come to take him, rises in a startling crescendo of appeal:

> Abate,—Cardinal,—Christ,—Maria,—God,—
> Pompilia, will you let them murder me?

2

Two main themes stand out from this massive poem. One is the worth of the human soul; the other is God's over-ruling purpose of love.

Browning never thought meanly of human worth and destiny.

THE RING AND THE BOOK

Great issues were at stake in every soul. He called men to courage and effort and urged upon them the importance of the right decision. There is no room for neutrality: 'life's business being just the terrible choice.' 'Side by side with his doctrine that there is no failure, no wretchedness or corruption that does not conceal within it a germ of goodness, is his sense of the evil of sin, of the infinite earnestness of man's moral warfare, and of the surpassing magnitude of the issues at stake for each individual soul. So powerful is his interest in man as a moral agent that he sees naught else in the world of any deep concern.'[1]

Two passages from the Pope's soliloquy will serve to illustrate this consciousness of mighty issues.

> Pompilia wife, and Caponsacchi priest,
> Are brought together as nor priest nor wife
> Should stand, and there is passion in the place,
> Power in the air for evil as for good,
> Promptings from heaven and hell, as if the stars
> Fought in their courses for a fate to be.
> Thus stand the wife and priest, a spectacle,
> I doubt not, to unseen assemblage there.
> No lamp will mark that window for a shrine,
> No tablet signalize the terrace, teach
> New generations which succeed the old
> The pavement of the street is holy ground;
> No bard describe in verse how Christ prevailed
> And Satan fell like lightning!

The other passage is more familiar and frequently quoted and has been given more fully already.[2]

> Was the trial sore?
> Temptation sharp? Thank God a second time!
> Why comes temptation but for man to meet

[1] Henry Jones, *op. cit.*, p. 117.
[2] See p. 91.

> And master and make crouch beneath his feet
> And so be pedestalled in triumph?

Browning believed that this was no unassisted struggle. God has made this world as a nursery of souls, and He has not left it. This is the faith expressed by the Pope, not lightly, but in full remembrance of the tragedy he is judging, and other like tragedies. As he studies nature he sees full evidence of God's power and wisdom, and in Christ he finds evidence that convinces heart and reason that in him there is also 'love without a limit'. This 'Christian tale' reveals to the Pope that true meaning of life. It is worth quoting his words once more:

> Beyond the tale, I reach into the dark,
> Feel what I cannot see, and still faith stands:
> I can believe this dread machinery
> Of sin and sorrow, would confound me else,
> Devised,—all pain, at most expenditure
> Of pain by Who devised pain,— to evolve,
> By new machinery in counterpart,
> The moral qualities of man—how else?—
> To make him love in turn and be beloved,
> Creative and self-sacrificing too,
> And thus eventually God-like.

Death does not mark the end of God's work upon the soul. Even for Guido, says the faith of the Pope and of Pompilia alike, there may be hope of remaking; though Caponsacchi seems to picture him as destined for annihilation.

To hold firmly on the one hand to the reality of the moral struggle, and on the other hand to the ultimate victory of the good, to the independence of the human soul and to the overruling Providence of God, is no easy faith; but Browning will not compromise on either hand. For him, love is God's last but sufficient word.

After the publication of *The Ring and the Book* Browning had twenty active years ahead of him, with a now firmly established standing as a poet. During those later years he wrote many fine poems, but never again touched such heights as here.

VIII

His Reverie

Never doubted clouds would break,
Never dreamed, though right were worsted, wrong would triumph.

Asolando

Browning was fond of putting 'Epilogues' at the close of his volumes, often deeply felt lyrics 'unlocking his heart' on some great issue. I can think of no better Epilogue for this study of the man and his work than to quote some portions from one of his very last poems. *Asolando* was published on the day he died. Almost the last poem in it is *Reverie*, a musing, as the title implies, over his long life and what it has meant to him. It is very characteristic of the consistent teaching of his religious and ethical works. He has seen good struggling with evil and love impotent to conquer wrong. Reason cannot solve the problem but faith remains. He is sure the day of Love's triumph is yet to come.

> As the record from youth to age
>   Of my own, the single soul—
> So the world's wide book: one page
>   Deciphered explains the whole
> Of our common heritage . . .
>
> Acquainted with joy and woe,
>   I could say 'Thus much is clear,
> Doubt annulled thus much: I know.

HIS REVERIE

'All is effect of cause:
   As it would, has willed and done
Power: and my mind's applause
   Goes, passing laws each one,
To Omnipotence, lord of laws.'

Head praises, but heart refrains
   From loving's acknowledgment.
Whole losses outweigh half-gains:
   Earth's good is with evil blent:
Good struggles but evil reigns.

Yet since Earth's good proved good—
   Incontrovertibly
Worth loving—I understood
   How evil—did mind descry
Power's object to end pursued—

Were haply as cloud across
   Good's orb, no orb itself . . .

. . . Past mind's conception—Power!
   Do I seek how star, earth, beast,
Bird, worm, fly, gained their dower
   For life's use, most and least?
Back from the search I cower . . .

Even as the world its life,
   So have I lived my own—
Power seen with Love at strife,
   That sure, this dimly shown,
—Good rare and evil rife.

Whereof the effect be—faith
   That, some far day, were found
Ripeness in things now rathe,
   Wrong righted, each chain unbound,
Renewal born out of scathe . . .

>   Then life is—to wake not sleep,
>   Rise and not rest, but press
>   From earth's level where blindly creep
>   Things perfected, more or less,
>   To the heaven's height, far and steep,
>
>   Where, amid what strifes and storms
>   May wait the adventurous quest,
>   Power is Love—transports, transforms
>   Who aspired from worst to best,
>   Sought the soul's world, spurned the worms'.
>
>   I have faith such end shall be:
>   From the first, Power was—I knew.
>   Life has made clear to me
>   That, strive but for closer view,
>   Love were as plain to see.
>
>   When see? When there dawns a day,
>   If not on the homely earth,
>   Then yonder, worlds away,
>   Where the strange and new have birth,
>   And Power comes full in play.

Browning was passing the proofs of *Asolando* in the last weeks of his life. When he had finished *Reverie* he came to the last poem of all, the *Epilogue*, and paused over its central verses:

>   What had I on earth to do
>   With the slothful, with the mawkish, the unmanly?
>   Like the aimless, helpless, hopeless, did I drivel
>   —Being—who?
>
> One who never turned his back but marched breast forward,
>   Never doubted clouds would break,
> Never dreamed, though right were worsted, wrong would triumph,
> Held we fall to rise, are baffled to fight better,
>   Sleep to wake.

HIS REVERIE

He read them out to his sister and daughter-in-law, who were in the room, and remarked: 'It almost sounds like bragging to say this, and as if I ought to cancel it; but it's the simple truth, and as it's true it shall stand.'

A SELECTION OF BOOKS ON ROBERT BROWNING

Out of the large literature I should pick these as the most interesting and useful.

The Poetical Works of Robert Browning, Edited by Augustine Birrell. First issued 1896, John Murray.

Mainly Biographical

W. Sharp, *Life of Robert Browning*, Walter Scott, 1890.

Mrs Sutherland Orr, *Life*, Revised edition, Murray, 1908.

Edward Dowden, *Life*, Dent (Everyman Library), 1904.

W. H. Griffin and H. C. Minchin, *Life*, Methuen, 1910. Revised 1938.

Betty Miller, *Robert Browning: A Portrait*, Murray, 1952.

G. B. Taplin, *Life of Elizabeth Barrett Browning*, Murray, 1957.

Letters

Letters of Robert Browning and Elizabeth Barrett, 1845–46, Murray, 1899.

Letters of Robert Browning, edited by T. L. Hood, Murray, 1933.

New Letters of Robert Browning, edited by W. C. De Vane and K. L. Knickerbocker, Murray, 1951.

Critical

Introduction to the Study of Browning. Arthur Symons. Dent, 1880. Revised edition, 1906.

Browning as a Philosophical and Religious Teacher. Henry Jones. Nelson, 1891.

The Reputation of Robert Browning. D. C. Somervell. Essays and Studies of the English Association. 1929.

A Browning Handbook. W. C. De Vane. Murray. 1935.

J. M. Cohen, *Robert Browning*, Longmans, 1952.

John Bryson, *Robert Browning*, Longmans, 1959.

INDEXES

I · POEMS BY ROBERT BROWNING, QUOTED AND DISCUSSED

Abt Vogler, 63, 100f.
Any Wife to Any Husband, 46
Apparent Failure, 93
Asolando, 39, 61, 104f., 120
At the Mermaid, 18, 88

Bells and Pomegranates, 17
Bishop Blougram's Apology, 52, 63
Blot in the 'Scutcheon, A, 19
By the Fireside, 33

Caliban upon Setebos, 53
Childe Roland, 12
Christmas Eve, 19, 23, 41f., 54f., 63, 71ff., 90
Cleon, 96ff.
Colombe's Birthday, 19
Cristina, 52

Death in the Desert, A, 41, 56, 63, 67ff.
Development, 26
Dramatis Personae, 81f., 103

Easter Day, 19, 41, 52, 71, 76ff.

Fears and Scruples, 89
Ferishtah's Fancies, 19, 39, 41, 45, 59ff., 90
Fifine at the Fair, 10, 18, 54, 93, 106
Fra Lippo Lippi, 21

Gold Hair, 90
Grammarian's Funeral, A, 99

House, 18

Ixion, 45

Karshish, An Epistle of, 41, 63, 65ff.

La Saisiaz, 19, 41f., 51, 101ff.
Last Ride Together, The, 63

Men and Women, 9, 33

One Word More, 19, 33f.

Pachiarotto, 11
Paracelsus, 19, 21f., 28, 48f., 56ff., 95f.
Parleyings, 23, 39, 41, 51, 91
Pauline, 18, 28
Pippa Passes, 22f., 84ff.

125

Prince Hohenstiel-Schwangau, 10, 49
Prospice, 13, 104

Rabbi ben Ezra, 51, 91f., 98f.
Reverie, 120ff.
Ring and the Book, The, 7, 14, 19, 33, 38, 41, 46f., 55, 64, 83, 87, 91, 99, 106ff.

Saul, 19, 25, 41, 51, 55, 63f., 91
Sordello, 10, 29, 50
Strafford, 19, 29

Toccata of Galuppi's, A, 63

Up at a Villa, 63

INDEXES

II · THE BROWNINGS

Elizabeth Barrett, 16, 29ff., 32ff., 37, 43
Robert Browning's Life,
  death and burial in the Abbey, 40
  early poems, 28
  education, 26f.
  Elizabeth's death, 36
  established fame, 37ff.
  introduction to Elizabeth Barrett, 29f.
  Italy, 29, 32f.
  life in Florence, 35f.
  marriage, 32ff.
  parents, 25ff.
  return to London, 36ff.
  Robert Barrett Browning, 33, 36f.
  visit to Russia, 28
Robert Browning's personality and work,
  dramatist, 19ff.
  humour, 11
  'message', 7, 13ff., 17ff., 54–62
  music, 26f., 36, 99f.
  nature, 21ff.
  obscurity, 8f., 12
  'optimism', 83ff.
  puritanism, 45
  religion *passim* and 19, 26, 41ff., 54ff., 82, 94, 95f., 101ff., 115, 118, 120ff.
  style, 7, 10f., 13
  'Victorianism', 8, 47

III · GENERAL

Abercrombie, Lascelles, 42, 87

Bryson, John, 9
Bunyan, 13

Carlyle, 8, 16, 28, 109
Cohen, J. M., 42

Dante, 96, 101
De Vane, 12f.
Dickens, 8, 28
Donne, 11

Eliot, T. S., 10
Essays and Reviews, 48, 90
Evolution, 48ff.

Forster, John, 28
Fox, W. J., 28

Griffin, W. H., 25

Hardy, Thomas, 8, 53, 89
Hawthorne, Nathaniel, 35

Inge, Dean, 45, 83

Jones, Henry, 16, 48, 117
Jowett, Benjamin, 38

Keats, 50
Kenyon, John, 29, 35

Landor, 28
Lucas, F. L., 83

Macready, 19
Maurice, F. D., 45
Miller, Mrs Betty, 39, 44
Milton, 15, 17

Orr, Mrs Sutherland, 19, 43f., 62, 82, 103

Renan, 48, 82
Ruskin, 9

Shakespeare, 17f., 92
Sharp, W., 16, 27
Shelley, 14ff., 27, 56
Somervell, D. C., 24
Spenser, 15
Stephen, Leslie, 16
Strauss, 48
Swinburne, 9
Symons, Arthur, 20

Taplin, G. B., 29, 33
Temple, William, 34, 42, 67
Tennyson, 8, 10f.

Victorian era, 47

Wordsworth, 8, 21

The SCM Book Club

BULLETIN 157
NOVEMBER 1963
SCM Book Club
635 East Ogden Avenue
Naperville, Illinois

From the Editor's Desk

Club Subscription Increase

American members who enrol through Alec R. Allenson need not read this! But I am afraid that all other members of the Club must be told now about an increase in subscriptions, coming into effect on 1 January 1964. The new rate will be 24s a year if you collect your books from a bookseller, or 28s a year if your books are sent from our London office (post free to any part of the world). This means that the books will now be 4s each to members, and 9s 6d to the public. But of course if you send your subscription before the end of 1963, the old rate will apply until your subscription is due for renewal.

The subscription was last raised in 1956. Since that date all our costs have climbed: postage, printing, paper, rent and staff. The cost of living in Britain has increased by 21%. We have struggled hard to delay this price increase (the new covers helped in 1959), but it has now become absolutely inevitable, and we hope for your understanding co-operation.

When the Club was founded in 1937, a book cost a member 2s. This would be over 6s today. The subscription had to be raised in 1947 and again in 1951, each time by 3s a year, the present increase.

The Free Book

offered to all who enrol a new member in November or December (please think about a Club subscription at the old rate as a Christmas gift!) is *The Day of His Coming*, a major new study of Jesus of Nazareth by Professor Gerhard Gloege who is now at Bonn University but who wrote this book in Communist East Germany.

The January Book

will be *Meeting the Orthodox Churches*, and will be illustrated. Its author is Herbert Waddams, who after work as General Secretary of the Church of England Council on Foreign Relations, and as a parish priest in Canada, is now a Canon of Canterbury Cathedral.

For some years now members have been asking for a book about the Eastern Orthodox Churches. We see photographs of their bearded bishops joining the World Council of Churches, we read of how their leaders collaborate with the Soviet government in Russia or drive the British out of Cyprus, perhaps we visit Orthodox churches in London or America—and we wonder! We didn't want a starry-eyed book, and this one is not in the least bit sentimental. But we wanted a book which had grown out of a love for the spiritual splendour of these ancient Christian bodies at their best. Canon Waddams interprets the Orthodox out of love, and sees many possibilities in the new meeting of East and West in the Church of Christ.

The March Book

will be by Dr Karl Barth. Considering that many people reckon Dr Barth the greatest theologian to appear since Calvin, or even since Aquinas, it is high time that we had a book by him in our series! His subject is practical: *Prayer and Preaching*.

Note for American Members

Since this material is already published in the USA (as two separate books, *Prayer* and *The Preaching of the Gospel* obtainable from Westminster Press), American members of the SCM Book Club who do *not* wish to receive a copy of the British edition of *Prayer and Preaching* next January are asked to notify Alec R. Allenson before 15 December. They will be sent as an alternative selection a new book by a Baptist scholar from Oxford University, Principal R. L. Child, entitled *A Conversation about Baptism*.

David L. Edwards

Hugh Martin

was Editor of the Religious Book Club from its foundation in 1937 to 1950—and therefore needs no introducing to the quite large numbers who joined the Club in those years and still belong. Perhaps still on your shelves are his RBC books *Christian Reunion*, *Great Christian Books*, *Luke's Portrait of Jesus* and *The Lord's Prayer*. More recently, he has edited for us the *Christian Treasury* series of classics.

He was born in 1890 and educated in Glasgow (he is an honorary Glasgow DD). He joined both the Baptist ministry and the staff of the Student Christian Movement in 1914. When the SCM Press was formed as a company in 1929 it was natural that he—who had already been in charge of the Movements' publications—should become its first Editor and Managing Director, until 1950. During the second world war he held a senior position in the Ministry of Information, and other public work has included the moderatorship of the Free Church Federal Council. He was made a Companion of Honour in 1955. He lives in retirement at East Grinstead in Sussex, but is still a Director of the SCM Press.

Kenneth Slack writes

Mr Slack is General Secretary of the British Council of Churches.

There seems something not a little ludicrous in writing about Hugh Martin in the bulletin of the Religious Book Club, of which he was the chief begetter. Such, however, is his inordinate modesty and capacity for self-effacement that not everyone will realize how immense and diverse have been the services of Dr Hugh Martin to the whole Church of God.

In the context within which I write, we think of him as editor and author. The list of his own writings reveals unusual catholicity of interest and knowledge alike. I suspect this present book has been a joy to write, for he once confessed to me that he was a teacher of English literature who happened to have taken a different turning. It is characteristic of his capacity for having his ear to the ground that he recognizes the likely contemporary reaction to a book on *The Faith of Robert Browning* (see page 7).

In the field of ecumenical thought and action Hugh Martin is second only to the veteran J. H. Oldham in the length of his experience and depth of his knowledge. The Glasgow student who sat entranced in the gallery at the World Missionary Conference at Edinburgh in 1910 became the chairman of the executive of COPEC in 1924, and one of the greatest leaders of the British Council of Churches.

And readers of this month's choice will recognize that ecclesiastical chores did not limit the breadth of his reading, nor ecumenical jargon corrupt the clarity of his style.

H. C. A. Gaunt writes

Mr Gaunt has recently been in charge of the teaching of English literature at Winchester College. An Anglican priest, he was formerly Headmaster of Malvern College.

The challenge of pessimism has been with us long enough. It is time we faced the challenge of optimism. We have emerged bloody but unbowed from T. S. Eliot's *Waste Land*; are we strong enough, and honest enough, to face the consequences of Browning's *The Ring and the Book*? Browning is not a poet to be interviewed over the toast and tea. He was (to use his own words) one who

> Never doubted clouds would break;
> Never dreamed, though right were worsted, wrong would triumph,
> Held we fall to rise, are baffled to fight better, sleep to wake.

He had a great deal to say, and in a great many poems, about the eternal purpose of God, the Divinity of Christ, the mystery of evil, life after death. But can we seriously believe that he has anything relevant to say to Arnold Wesker, or the Bishop of Woolwich, or the BBC television wits of *That Was the Week That Was*, when he is capable of writing,

> *God's in His heaven: all's right with the world?*

Hugh Martin deals as effectively with this popular misconception of what Browning meant by the above quotation (in pages 83 to 88) as he fastens unerringly on the main ideas and 'message' (horrible word—as he records George Wyndham's saying). The chapter (only 13 pages) on *The Ring and the Book* is express and admirable. He quotes D. C. Somervell's apt remark, written in 1929, 'We shall be noted—among other things—for the strange fact that we could not appreciate Browning'. I have been teaching intelligent Sixth Formers the poetry of Robert Browning for the last thirty years. I only wish there had been as good a short book to commend to them long ago.

Speaking about God

In his new book of sermons *The Eternal Now* (SCM Press, 16*s*; Scribner's, New York), Paul Tillich says:

Must we spread silence around what concerns us more than anything else—the meaning of our existence? The answer is—no! For God himself has given mankind names for himself in those moments when he has broken into our finitude and made himself manifest. We can, and must use these names. For silence has power only if it is the other side of speaking, and in this way becomes itself a kind of speaking. This necessity is both our justification and our being judged, when we gather together in the name of God. We are an assembly where we speak about God. We are a church. The church is the place where the mystery of the holy should be experienced with awe and sacred embarrassment. But is this our experience? Are our prayers, communal or personal, a use or a misuse of the divine name? Do we feel the sublime embarrassment that so many people outside the churches feel? Are we gripped by awe when, as ministers, we point to the Divine Presence in the sacraments? Or, as theological interpreters of the holy, are we too sure that we can really explain him to others? Is there enough sacred embarrassment in us when fluent Biblical quotations or quick, mechanized words of prayer pour from our mouths? Do we preserve the respectful distance from the Holy-Itself, when we claim to have the truth about him, or to be at the place of his Presence or to be the administrators of his Power—the proprietors of the Christ? How much embarrassment, how much awe is alive in Sunday devotional services all over the world?

And now let me ask the Church and all its members, including you and myself, a bold question. Could it be that, in order to judge the misuse of his name within the Church, God reveals himself from time to time by creating silence about himself? Could it be that sometimes he prevents the use of his name in order to protect his name, that he withholds from a generation what was natural to previous generations—the use of the word God? Could it be that godlessness is not caused only by human resistance, but also by God's paradoxical action—using men and the forces by which they are driven to judge the assemblies that gather in his name and take his name in vain? Is the secular silence about God that we experience everywhere today perhaps God's way of forcing his Church back to a sacred embarrassment when speaking of him? It may be bold to ask such questions. Certainly there can be no answer, because we do not know the character of the divine providence. But even without an answer, the question itself should warn all those inside the Church to whom the use of his name comes too easily.

OUR BEST RECOMMENDATION

ONE MEMBER ENROLLING ANOTHER

(*A copy of the current free book listed in the SCM Book Club bulletin will be sent from London to each member enrolling others.*)

SCM Book Club
P.O. Box 31, Naperville, Illinois.

☐ For $5.40 enclosed enrol my friend.

Name ....

Address..

City .... Zone............State......
   ☐ *OR send information to above address.*

☐ Please send GIFT CARD.

☐ Send free book for enrolling above new member.

☐ Send me.........descriptive circulars and order cards for group subscriptions, at reduced rates.

☐ Enter my personal subscription or ☐ renewal.

☐ 1 year, six books every two months. $5.40.

My name..

Address..

City........................... Zone............ State......

Printed in Great Britain by Billing and Sons Ltd., Guildford and London